SoLoMo Success

SoLoMo Success

Social Media, Local and Mobile Small Business Marketing Strategy Explained

Ray Sidney-Smith
W3 Publishing
2014

SoLoMo Success - Social Media, Local and Mobile Small Business Marketing Strategy Explained by Ray Sidney-Smith

 Ray Sidney-Smith is a perennial Small Business Evangelist, speaker, strategist and author, working tirelessly to help small businesses launch, grow and succeed in the marketplace each and every day.

He is also the President of W3 Consulting (www.w3cinc.com), a consultancy providing consulting, seminar presentations and workshops to small businesses, non-profit/community-based organizations, and small-to-solo law firms throughout the United States with practical approaches to business development using Web, Social Media, mobile and digital technologies.

Books may be purchased by contacting the publisher or author at:

http://w3cinc.com/contact/
ray@w3cinc.com

Cover Design: Sam Cusano
Publisher: W3 Publishing
Editor: Raymond Sidney-Smith (Editing by Ray)
First Edition
10 9 8 7 6 5 4 3 2 1

Table of Contents

Part I - Content Marketing and the SoLoMo Connection

Chapter 1: Old Way Versus New Way

"Everybody gets so much
information all day long that they
lose their common sense."

~Gertrude Stein

The world's first newspaper, the *Relation* (a
German publication beginning in 1605 AD),
marks a major shift in the way in which
humans were exposed to and consumed
information. If you can even imagine a time
when the world lacked a way for you to
access news information other than by letter,
official documents from your government
(typically a monarch in the centuries
surrounding the invention of the printing
press) posted in town centers, or word of
mouth. Now, in modern times, we all are

bombarded with information to the point where I hear complaints frequently about the onslaught of media and the advertising that supports the news industry. While we can look to (and thank) the traditional print journalism community as the beginning of the democratization of information, we can also look to them as the paradigm of an old way of thinking about the dissemination of information. What is this Old Way? Well, it is the idea that you push information at people in one direction. Just as mechanical movable type printing altered the course of society forever, the Internet (the technology infrastructure digitally connecting us together) and the subsequent and ongoing publishing of billions of pages on the World Wide Web mark a seismic shift in the way in which humans produce, consume and engage with information and one another.

Historians will look back on this Digital Age as rudimentary but also with awe at the speed of this significant advance in the communications of society. Stop and think about it: the Internet and World Wide Web are only about 25 years old! Think about all of the other industries **ever** in the history of industrialized nations. They advanced in baby steps and did not see nearly what we are seeing evolve in the proliferation of Web, digital and electronics technologies. Twenty years into creation of the automobile gave us the Ford *Model T*! So, what is the New Way? I should really say that there are the New Ways, since so many advancements are happening on a consistent, concurrent basis it is tough for even the savviest, technology-oriented people to follow. At its core, the New Way is that instead of the pushing information at people in one direction, the media, business (including your small business) and **everyone else** can now co-create and engage in a conversation digitally, virtually. Additionally, in order to truly understand the power of this simple paradigm shift in content creation, we need to understand a bit of science...about ourselves and how we interact. In the sciences, we have Psychology (studying the mind's function and its manifestation in human behavior) and Sociology (that which studies the social interactions of humans) to help us understand why the New Way evolved.

Understanding the Buyer

In general, psychology and sociology have told us many important things about humans and society. Several of them apply to this discussion of the New Way and hopefully will help lay the groundwork for your marketing strategy now and long into the future. I am going to give some generalizations so that we are on the same page; this is far from academic but these are important enough understandings about who we are and how we operate with one another. First, we thrive on getting together in groups; it is engrained in our nature. Next, people like to broaden the size of their social groups but not too much; each group is unique in that there is a "this feels right" range. When you have more or less than that appropriate number, things start to fizzle or become unwieldy. And, finally, we buy in an ever-changing series of mindsets, not some static perspective that might be the perception from the way that an advertising sales executive might characterize his consumer audience.

Let us take a book club as an example about social groups to understand my first two points. I find it remarkable that people do not read more books by and large, yet there are thousands of book clubs created and running every year on every genre under the sun. People *buy* books though; it's an intellectual status symbol. And, the few that read those books want to organize in reading groups, get together and talk about them. In my years of running several book clubs, the ideal number for a book club is about 8 to 12 members attending any particular reading discussion meeting. If you have any more people than that, it can be difficult for everyone's opinions to be heard and to keep people from starting side conversations. If you have fewer than eight people (and especially if they happen to be less than social) then the conversation may get stale or forced and members are not as likely to return for future book club meetings. You have to look at successful communities like the one you (which you will realize by reading this book) want to create, to see what kinds of numbers work for those groups and to manage your marketing to get your community size within that range.

People operate also on needs and wants as it relates to buying products and services, as you have probably read in countless business marketing books and Web articles. It is important to understand this in the context of what needs and wants fit where, for your customer. I tend to look at this from the format of the great American psychologist Abraham H. Maslow's Hierarchy of Needs. Your business fits somewhere among the levels of the Hierarchy of Needs, and it is a good exercise to think about where your product/service fits. As the pyramid diagram below shows, there are varying strata of needs and wants for humans. In my business management perspective, as one looks *upward* from lower on the pyramid he or she desires less needs and more wants. Counter-intuitively, as one looks *downward* from higher on the pyramid she or he sees less value of needs and more value of wants. On the one hand, if I am struggling to make ends meet, I dream about owning a red Aston Martin sports car, having the perfect spouse/partner and children, and receiving a call that my 15th *New York Times* best-selling book just broke a million sales. Conversely, when I am feeling really successful in my life, I tend toward avoiding thinking about the trivialities and I think more about my next vacation, doing something philanthropic for my community, or starting a new, exciting business venture. All this together translates that wants outweigh needs to the human mind, especially in a rich nation like the United States.

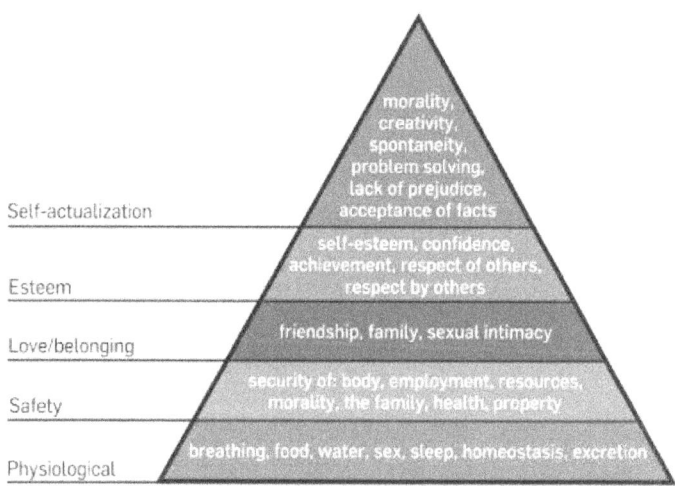

Abraham H. Maslow's Hierarchy of Needs

In simplest terms, it is relatively easy to sell commodity-based products at the foundational level of the pyramid; however, there is also strong competition there and a business needs to differentiate on customer service, pricing strategy, and value-added benefits. Meanwhile, as you reach the zenith of the pyramid, it's equally easier to sell luxury services since someone operating at that level has (presumably) the desire and ability to buy them; however, there is equally strong competition at that level, and a business that wants to compete successfully in that market must communicate values, be superior in responsiveness, and innovate where their client does not expect it. What's missing here? The people in the middle are, of course.

I am going to take the wild guess that most of you reading this are somewhere in the middle: you're not impoverished nor are you filthy rich. And, that means your mindset fluctuates up and down the needs and wants spectrum from wanting some luxury items at times to needing some basic necessities at others. Why do I explain all this that seems so plainly obvious? As Gertrude Stein said, we are bombarded with information daily which tends to befuddle us, and I think we forget that people's needs and wants change on a regular basis. And, you need to be adapting to the changing patterns along with your potential and valued customers! Too often I find that business owners stagnate in their marketing strategy. "This is the way it's always worked, Ray!" Well, as a good friend was told once, "You're a smart person, and fully capable of running your business into the ground." Do not think the Old Way is the right way to succeed today; think of it as shooting a limited numbers of arrows (your marketing and advertising budget) at a target in pitch-black darkness. The New Way is a moving target, yes—and does mean that it is tougher to hit bulls-eyes as often—but thankfully you can see the targets today and have many more arrows (your content, your customers, and your marketing and advertising budget combined) than ever before.

How will you engage your buyers to get together and discuss your products or services, even though they may or may not always be buying from you, and keep the conversation interesting and lively with everyone's fluctuating moods? Well, to accomplish that you will definitely need to get creative (to which I can recommend only to watch John Cleese's YouTube video on creativity [http://youtu.be/tmY4-RMB0YY]), and you will need to learn a strategy for how to utilize the technologies of the New Way. Regarding the New Way's technologies and strategy, I can help you there: so read on and invest in yourself by learning these concepts and installing them into your small business. The journey begins.

Chapter 2: Community - Give. Get. Belong.

"A community is like a ship;
everyone ought to be prepared to
take the helm."

~Henrik Ibsen

As I said in Chapter 1, humans have needs; three core needs to be exact: to give, to get, and feel a sense of belonging. It is the primary reason you are a part of any group of people, whether it is your family, your friend network, your church, or your business. In each of those environments, you give, get or feel a sense of belonging. And, if you have all three needs met in any group, there is a pretty strong bond among the members. Not all group members have all three needs satisfied, but we know the more of them that are there the better the group dynamics. Below I have defined how these parts of human need translate on the Web, first through how giving, getting and feeling like one belongs affect us, and then what you do as a Web community manager (which is what every Small Business owner is today).

Giving

When I use the word "give," I do not necessarily mean philanthropy, tithing or charity. The term really means to offer something without an expectation of getting anything in exchange. We give out of a desire to serve others.

Getting

We start out our lives in our mothers' wombs. We took nourishment from her until birth, and received all that we needed in those tender moments in our new lives. During that period, you were "getting." You have ebbs and flows in life when you need to get (or take) things from others. And, the people who give to you are doing it under the auspices of "giving" that I defined above. They are not looking to get something from you explicitly or as payment for service or product; there is an understood relationship between givers and receivers in communities that sometimes you need to give and sometimes you need to take. And, it is for the good of the group.

Belonging

Back to our mothers' wombs, there is a point when we are all born. And, it's at this point that you are made to feel a sense of belonging. This is very powerful, and those who do not get these early, important stimuli can be irreparable harmed for life. Once we are adults, we do not really ever lose that desire to feel a sense of belonging, and we seek that in groups. In this way, we build social equity among members of groups through connecting with each other and making others feel welcome within the group.

Translating This to Small Business Activities

At this juncture, you need to take giving,

getting and belonging to the activities you need to be doing in your Web presence management to effectuate the strategy. I use the simple yet immensely effective strategy of Listen, Speak and Connect.

Listening to Give What's Needed and Wanted

This is the initial phase of any business communications strategy. In essence, you listen actively for what your target audience (potential, current and past customers), industry experts, colleagues, competition, and vendors from around the country are saying about you (individually), your business, and your industry, their needs and what's happening, respectively. Through active listening, we can learn key insights about your business that you could not know otherwise, respond to them and their needs/wants, and adapt nimbly to the needs of your target audience and the changing business landscape. Clue: many times what you'll learn that your customers want is not necessarily your product/service but valuable information and experiences with your product/service bundled up in it.

Speaking to Get the Web Traffic Your Business Needs

Next, you create an editorial calendar (thinking like a magazine publisher does about publishing their periodicals on a schedule) based on broad and specific themes that cater to your audience. In that editorial calendar you can plan out what content you will produce, publish for your target audience and to what Web properties (website "Resources" or "Articles" page, blog, social networking sites, and more). Most of the content will be curated content from other sources and then a portion of that content is that which you as a Small Business blogger will be create (which we'll get to later). Always with your own content, the goal is drive traffic from Social Media to your website (which we'll get to later also).

Connecting to Create the Glue to Your Community

Just as referrals are the lifeblood of Small

Business, you must work the power of the crowd to make great connections with the social influencers within your target audience, among your target audience, and among your industry colleagues. This will create a stronger community for engagement as well as provide the all-important feedback loop mechanism needed so that you can focus inside and outside with your learning, responding and adapting practice of active listening.

Measure What You Can

With all of the above, you must begin tracking everything you are doing on the Web so that you can review on a regular basis the success and learning opportunities of your online activities in an iterative approach (as opposed to a classical sequential, progressive approach) to success. This data is vital to succeed in building a stronger community, how to convert curated content into self-generated content of interest to our target audience, and internal content to better formats and more specific topics to engage our target audience in those verticals.

All told, your goal in all of our communications is to listen carefully, be transparent, be responsive, be authentic, and tell the great stories that your business has to offer.

I BROODED Over Every Article I Wrote

Considering I discussed publishing under *Speaking* above, I think it is appropriate to clue you in on an efficient method for publishing on a schedule. We all have only so much time in our days for marketing and management, as well as getting the "business of the business" accomplished every day. Therefore, I follow a publishing process I've coined "BROODED" that I use in my content production when I'm producing any kind of content (specifically for me it is mostly to help me manage the ghost-blogging process for my clients since it's collaborative).

BROODED stands for:

- **B**rainstorm

- **R**esearch

- **O**rganize & **O**utline

- **D**raft

- **E**dit

- **D**isseminate (Publish & Syndicate)

The reason behind this is so that I can chunk similar tasks together to be more efficient with my time, as well as be able to delegate portions of the content production to others internally. I tend to Brainstorm in sessions about a variety of different content and themes. Yes, I capture ideas when they come to me. But, there is nothing like spending a finite period of open time without anything else distracting me to think up great ideas for what I'd like to produce that would be appealing to my intended audience. Next, the Research phase is where I find out what others are saying about—for or against— online and in other offline research sources (e.g., periodicals, books, and scholarly research databases). This may bring me back to Brainstorm more, if needed. Then, I spend the effort to Organize & Outline the titles of posts, vetting what research I am going to use, and writing out a basic outline of my thesis statement, opening/introduction, body points and conclusion. Further, I Draft and Edit the posts usually in blocks of time according to theme so that I'm more or less writing series of posts. The process goes from drafting and then putting that drafted content into a state of hibernation for me to review at a later time when I've had enough time to distance myself from the ideas. Finally, I Disseminate (that is, publish it publicly) the material in its redacted form and it gets syndicate properly to where I intend to expose the content to my audience.

Roles, Responsibilities & Responsible Parties

Now is a good time to explain the important roles as information givers in your business. Running a business is tough, and certainly adding a host of new work to your plate is daunting for some while an exciting challenge to others. To make investing in SoLoMo as practical and smooth as possible, I recommend that (even if you're a solopreneur) that you define the hats you're going to where and who is going to do which tasks throughout each marketing campaign.

Active Listener is responsible for receiving or seeking out conversations outlined under LISTEN above, respond according to guidelines in the ePolicy, send this data along to Measurement Analyst, and report back to the Communications Manager as necessary (such as for crisis communications) or requested. This will be several individuals within the organization working together to cover conversations that automated technology cannot alert us.

Communications Director, or "Community Manager" oversees the Social Media team, is responsible for training, and reports to the owner of the business. (Many times, it is the business owner.)

Content Producer's responsibilities will be a commitment to producing content for publication according to the editorial calendar the Social Media team assembles. All of the company's staff and independent consultants should be responsible for producing (or capturing) some form of content.

Syndicator is knowledgeable about the technical specifics of posting to each kind of Social Media, this role will post Content Producers' redacted, approved content to each active network on behalf of the business.

Moderators pass feedback and questions along to the appropriate party and is in charge of getting that response back to the appropriate person).

Measurement Analysts are responsible for collecting Web data and assembling reports for the Social Media team to review and discuss improving communications efforts over time.

Checklist

✓   Write a Digital Communications Policy (ePolicy) for your business. (This should take you no more than approximately 2-3 hours.) See the following Web resource for sample ePolicies for your business: *Online Database of Social Media Policies - Social Media Governance* [http://goo.gl/y1Zu]

✓   Assign someone or several people to each of the roles outlined in this chapter, except as I stated it's best to have one Community Manager. If you're a solopreneur, merge the Active Listener and Moderator roles, and plan to spend at least an hour in one of those roles every workday (and likely two hours as Content Producer). So, for example, Monday you would do you block out an hour as an Active Listener/Moderator for your brand/company/organization; Tuesday you'd block out an hour for looking at the bigger picture as Community Manager; Wednesday you would block out two hours as Content Producer to capture and develop your content; and so on.

Chapter 3: Web Presence: Your Website Is the Center of Your Small Business Universe

"When they discover the center of the universe, a lot of people will be disappointed to discover they are not it."

~Bernard Bailey

Web Presence

I know this will come back to haunt me someday, but I have an unquenchable thirst for cop shows. There, I said it. And, if you have watched as much *Law & Order*, *Criminal Minds*, and *CSI* as I have, you probably know all about "psychological profiling" of criminals. And, there is an entire field of law enforcement professionals (ergo, forensic criminologists and criminal psychologists) that spend their entire careers studying and identifying these mental traits. Well, this concept did not start with the mentally deranged committing heinous acts. It actually started with the founders of modern psychology (such as James, Tichtener, Freud, *et al*.) trying to understand a basic framework for how the mind operated. We have come a **long** way from those days and now we have marketing books, like the seminal work, *Positioning* by Al Ries and Jack Trout, which unveils the buyer's mind for the business marketer. And, just as your buyer has a psychological profile that others perceive and understand, it turns out that your business has an digital identity that is an extension of your brand. I call it your *Web presence*.

Web presence really has many different facets, just like your personal identity and how you perceive yourself (and how others see you). Your Web presence is everything you, your business and your employees do—whether regarding your product/service and brand messaging, or not—on the World Wide Web and beyond. It's your business' digital brand. And, your buyer is learning today that to understand your products/services, it should learn as much about your Web presence as possible before buying. And, they are learning this first through Social Media, Local Search results, and via Mobile Media.

Sitting in Traffic

Being stuck on the freeway coming home from work every day for nearly a decade at one of my past offices, it used to make me crazy that an 11-mile drive could take me nearly an hour going against the flow of rush-hour traffic. It never made sense to me and I could not imagine why I (or any of my fellow traffic dwellers) was doing this to myself. In contrast, I want you and your business to sit in traffic. No, I'm not a sadist. While it may seem counter-intuitive, you want to sit in the midst of *as much traffic* on the Information Superhighway as possible. This traffic brings people to your website, and your website is where sales happen. (I'll be repeating this phrase many times throughout the book...on purpose. It's that important to understand.) This may seem strange for you if you have not ever had a sale (or even a lead contact you) from your website yet. But, if you start to do the activities I profess here, you will begin to get those sales (and leads) from your website, so never fear.

The Birds and the Bees—The Basics of Making Traffic

It is good to have a basis of what it means to build good Web traffic for your business. This will help make the Social, Local and Mobile traffic options make much more sense as we get to those topics in later chapters. Again, this will help you know where to get started in your Search Strategy implementation, but more importantly be able to know how to ask the right questions of the Web professionals you partner with to build your business' Web presence.

These are the basic terms you should be

familiar with throughout your Web presence development:

ALT – Web code that you put in the *HTML* of your website with images that tell Search Engines what the picture is

Back Link – *Hyperlinks* that **others** put on their websites and social sites that direct people to your website

Bots (Robots, Crawlers, Spiders) – Software that *Search Engines* use to look at websites, see whether they are worthy of be included, and to check when they were last updated; the automated information analysts of the Web

Bounce Rate – how often someone visits your website and immediately leaves from one page on your website

CAPTCHA – the sometimes frustrating to consumers but extremely useful spam-prevention tool that requires the user to

type words or numbers shown in a
picture before submitting comments or
creating users on a website

Clicks – when someone presses a *hyperlink*
and is directed to a file or Web page

CSS (Cascade Style Sheets) – Web coding
that allows you to make changes to the
visual layout/design of your website
from an external file, therefore if you
make one change to *CSS* it happens
across the entire website (e.g., you can
say that all words that are in italics are
also changed to display in green Arial
12pt font)

DNS (Domain Name System) – method for
translating the words you know for
Domain Names (e.g.,
www.yourbusinessname.com) and *Web
addresses* (e.g.,
www.yourbusinessname.com/your-
really-great-content-with-
keywords.html) into their real location

on the *Internet.*

Domain Name (URL, URI, Web Address) –
letters, numbers and characters that
represent a location on the Web in a
better way that just fixed Internet
locations (known as IP addresses),
which are similar to a cartographer's
use of longitude and latitude on a map;
(e.g.,
http://www.yourbusinessname.com
directs you to http://192.168.1.0); this
makes it much easier to remember for
you and your customers, while still
letting Web servers and technical folks
to manage their world efficiently and
orderly; there are many rules about
Domain Names but primarily you will
be required to register domains with 3
to 67 characters, adhere to the LDH rule
(letters, numbers and hyphens only),
and have at least one letter (not all
numbers and hyphens), and choose one
of the domain extensions
(.COM, .BIZ, .US, .NET, .ORG, *et al.*)

Host (Web host, Web hosting service) – the service provider of online file storage that connects your *Domain Name* and *HTML* files on the Internet to a person's Web browser

HTML (HyperText Markup Language) – Web coding language that displays content and files on the Web to a person's Web browser

Hyperlink (Link) - the elevator buttons to the Internet, this is usually text that takes you to a new place or opens a file on the *World Wide Web*

ISP (Internet Service Provider) – the telecommunications company that provides a connection to the Internet from any point of service: consumer and *Host*.

Keywords / Key Phrase – a word (or sometimes a number or character) or series of words that you type into a *Search Engine* to find information

Meta data (Meta Tag, Meta Description, Meta Keywords, Meta Robots) – information you place in the *HTML* of your web pages so that *Search Engines* understand your website better

Pay Per Click (PPC/CPC), PPA, CPM, and CPI – pricing methodologies for online advertising; if you want to do any kind of online advertising, it behooves you to search Google for the above acronyms for full explanations

Registrar – company through which you "buy" (actually, it's a lease of) *Domain Names*; many times "Domain Host" is used when talking to Web professionals and vendors, but they actually mean the company where your Web hosting is located when you type in your Domain, not your Registrar

RSS (Rich Site Summary, commonly known as Really Simple Syndication) – vital Web technology that allows syndication

of your Web pages, most commonly
your blog posts

Search Engine / Directory – while these are
distinctly different entities, they are
websites that people search via
keywords or view categories to find
websites; *Search Engines* allow a
searcher up to 10 substantive words
(without the's, to's, an's and so on) so
that means you want to appeal to *Search
Engines* in less than 10 *keywords*

Search Engine Results Page (SERP) – the
Web pages displaying the results of
your *keyword* searches on a *Search
Engine*.

SEO (Search Engine Optimization) –
techniques for making your website
more appealing to be included in
Search Engines and Search Directories,
and being shown more often and
higher on SERPs

Site Analytics – information gathered by

software on your website about the Web *visitors*

Sitemap – file that websites publish in order to tell *Search Engines* about the file structure and location of Web pages and files on the website

Title – Web code that you put in the *HTML* of your website that displays the information in the Web browser tab

Visitors – while there are different varieties that *Site Analytics* report, these are the people (and sometimes Web software, like *bots*) coming to your website

White Hat – legitimate *SEO* techniques that will not get you penalized by *Search Engines* and *Search Directories*

World Wide Web (WWW) – the visible pages and files the general public can visit and consume information connected via the Internet

I'll give a brief introduction of how the *World Wide Web* developed so that you can see how the Web terminologies all work in combination. In 1990, Sir Tim Berners-Lee (a British computer scientist and engineer working at the prestigious Swiss-French-border scientific research organization, CERN) and his colleague, Robert Cailliau, developed the *hyperlink* as a means to connect all the disparate information on Web servers around the world (what we know as the Internet), thereby creating the World Wide Web. This amazing undertaking included many organizations (including ICANN, domain *registrars* and World Wide Web Consortium (W3C), of which Sir Berners-Lee is the long-time Director, and the global network of ISPs) to create the Web standards for *Domain Names*, *HTML*, and *CSS*. With these Web standards, individuals, companies and organizations were empowered to put more on the Web. *Search Directories* started to launch all over the Web with the hopes of making it easier to find information, thereby creating advertising opportunities (primarily *Pay Per Click* ads) alongside the submitted websites to the directories.

Meanwhile, a new breed of websites came online, *Search Engines*, attempting to provide a way to find websites directly from *keyword* popularity. And, so, *Search Engine Optimization (SEO)* was born and *Search Engines* had to start fighting against people trying to game their way of determining great, relevant content from just people making irrelevant pages that captured search traffic. Google (a *Search Directory* turned *Search Engine*) came up with a new search algorithm that used *keywords* and *clicks* different prominence in their *Search Engine.*

Google became a highly capable tool for the masses to use, giving them the opportunity to make huge amounts of *PPC/CPM* advertising revenue on their *Search Engine Results Pages*. Web professionals and publishers of websites have learned to hone their Web properties using hopefully only *White Hat* ways of getting noticed and displayed prominently on Google and the other major engines, using *Title*, *Meta data*, *hyperlinks*, *keywords*, *site analytics* and *sitemaps* to increase *visitors* and decrease *bounce rates*. And, with the advent of blogging and Social Media, *RSS* feeds have made it great to syndicate content across websites and increase *Search Engine* traffic. However, blogging created also tons of keyword abusers ("Web pirates" as I call them) that leave comments with just keywords that did not make sense to capture traffic so tools like *CAPTCHA*, working with your DNS, *Web host* and *ISPs* (to deal with larger Web pirate operations) developed to combat these ne'er-do-wells. And, so now, you know a brief history of the World Wide Web.

If you get lost on any term while you're learning about Web presence management for your company, never fear. Visit NetLingo and they'll define almost any term with which you are unfamiliar. (Webopedia also exists but I find their advertising distracting on the site.)

- http://netlingo.com

- http://webopedia.com

Intent

The overarching Web traffic strategy is to understand the intent of your potential customer when they go to Google (or another search engine), figure out the keywords that match your potential customers' intent, and create great content that you infuse your keywords in that content onto your website. More often than not you'll hear about creating "relevant content" for the Search Engines. I do not like that terminology because it does not really get at the heart of your business' connection to your customers. While I have my criticisms of the late Steve Jobs' management style, I agree with him on one thing: thinking from the perspective of your consumer will pay dividends to your business success. Get into their minds just like forensic criminologists and criminal psychologists. You should understand yourself well and your customers better! If you can anticipate your needs and wants on the Intent front then you can be ahead of your competitors and always impress your potential target market with your great content.

Keywords

To get a good idea about the keywords you should be using (but is by no means an absolute index of keywords), visit Google AdWords Keyword Planning Tool [http://adwords.google.com/select/KeywordT oolExternal/].

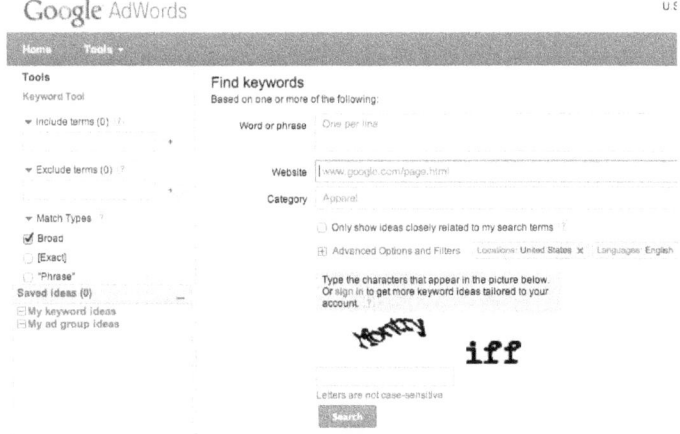

You may be required (if you're not logged into your Google user account) to input the CAPTCHA text (see the note above in yellow) so that they know you're not a robot, then click on the "Search" button.

	Competition	Global Monthly Searches	Local Monthly Searches
	Low	2,740,000	550,000
new galaxy s4	Medium	9,900	2,900
the new galaxy s4	Medium	9,900	2,900
galaxy 3 1	High	2,240,000	201,000
the galaxy s 4	Low	368,000	40,500
customizing pictures	Low	260	110
machalibs samsung	Low	260	110
google glasses	Low	12	< 10
social media submit	Low	8,100	4,400
galaxy s4 features	Low	8,100	1,300
new galaxy s 4	Low	3,600	1,800
ceo mashable	Low	320	140
the new samsung galaxy	Medium	165,000	33,100
galaxy s 3 review	High	40,500	12,100
galaxy s 3	High	1,830,000	301,000
samsung mashable	Low	260	110
video conference online	High	40,500	9,900
the market apps	Medium	201,000	49,500

What you'll return is a page with an option to download a spreadsheet of the results, of the top 100 keywords associated with your website.

If you do not have a website yet, pick your nearest and closest-related competitor's website(s) and see what keywords result from that search.

Domain Names and Short URLs

As we discussed earlier, capturing the Web traffic data for your website as well as your Social Media activity is very important to learning and growing your Web presence. You have your main business domain (typically, ending in .COM) but maybe not the other major domain name extensions (top-level domains, or "TLDs"); you should register the domains for at least: .NET, .ORG, .US, .BIZ and .INFO; these are the most prone to be used by cyber-squatters and those attempting to drive traffic away from your site to competitors' sites over time (or capture that traffic to monetize it through display advertising). Also, if your business has common misspellings, you should probably secure those misspelled domain names to direct to your website as well. Domain names are a very affordable defense mechanism for your business' hard-earned Web traffic. We used to recommend that you capture .MOBI (for mobile browser visitors) but it seems to have lost steam in the market and so you can just use yourbusiness.com/mobile if you intend on hosting a separate, mobile-friendly website under your domain. (Although m.yourbusinessname.com works technically just as well, it's not as liked by Google and the other major search engines so I would avoid it in practice.)

As well, we recommend that you develop a branded, short URL for your business to track the Social Media activity. Some examples are nytim.es (The New York Times), goo.gl (Google), fb.me and shar.es (both Facebook). The decision for the short URL you use has a couple of factors: length, brand and availability. There are some interesting customs that have developed around short URLs, such as adding ccTLDs (country code TLDs) such as "ly" (Libya), "it" (Italy) and "es" (Spain) to your name (such as bit.ly, visual.ly, vid.ly, dlvr.it, iTun.es, and so on). And, you can possible use the .CO extension with an abbreviation of your business name or product/service, if your business name does not lend well to the above customs is best (e.g., nwc.co). In doing so, people know you are a business and will connect the dots when they see the short URL. Tip: You want the branded, short URL to be set up in bit.ly PRO (or another similar service) and used for ALL hyperlinks you use in Social Media (Facebook,

Twitter, LinkedIn, Google+, Pinterest, your blog, and so on).

Build it or buy it

The next major decision you will need to decide on is whether to build your website yourself, hire a Web development/design firm, or use a pre-built Web service. Here are the issues you should consider and a comparison of the pro's and con's.

Website Considerations

Design
One of the first major considerations for launching your new website for your business is how you want your website to visually appeal to your target audience. This is a point of internal conflict for me as I believe aesthetics are important but not at the expense of your content and underlying infrastructure of your website. I know this will bring ire from creative professionals and those whose businesses are about design and aesthetics; you certainly need to pay attention

to your site's visual appeal considering your clients are judging you on that basis. However, the super majority of high traffic websites are not beautiful (think about Google; they're a white page with a logo and search field), they are extremely functional and competently navigable. I say all this so you do not get too hung up on trying to make your website aesthetically perfect and therefore delay its launch. I see this all the time so do not get caught in that trap.

So, in contemplation of your website, you can hire several different creative professionals to handle everything from the site's overall visual theme, your business logo as it will appear on the Web (and in Social Media) as it may be different than your printed version, photography that you'd be including on your Web pages, and buy now/sales buttons and other visual elements you may need. As I will discuss in the Development section below, there are many ways for you to do some or all of this work yourself if you have the time and desire to learn the skills and tools to create the visuals for your website.

Development – When you decide to develop a website your first step is to decide whether you are building what we call a static versus dynamic website. This means that if you are building a static website, it is just HTML files are manually created and edited on your Web host. When you want to make a change, you or your Web developer will open the Web coding files using software or the text files themselves and make the edits and re-upload those files over the prior ones. Comparatively, if you build the website using what's called a content management system (or, CMS) you will do all the editing of the website through a website back-end administration dashboard, not needing to know any kind of Web coding in order to get around adding new content (text, pictures and video) to the website after the developer hands over the site administration to you and your staff. I recommend that you go with a content management system such as WordPress, Drupal or Joomla.

Content – This is the first thing you should do, which is to outline the content you would like to have on the website. While your Web professional may help you with some of this, you may want to hire the services of a copywriter with a specialty in Web content. Additionally, you can hire someone to completely write your content for the initial website, but understand that you and your staff will still need to be creating new content. This will be content created over time after the site launches unless you plan on a long-term relationship with a copywriter (in which case you should make sure that's in your budget). Remember to spell-check using your Word processing software, spell-check manually, and then have someone else proofread also; everything you write to put on the website. Everything.

Maintenance – If you use a developer to assist you in launching your website, it's best that you make sure that your agreement with the developer include maintenance provisions. Software upgrades, training and assistance making minor upgrades over the time you plan to have that version of the website (typically 3-5 years) live. This could also include emergency provisions to monitor your website in case it goes down, and to troubleshoot those problems.

- http://wordpress.org

- http://drupal.org

- http://joomla.org

Function Over Form

Web design is a balancing act of several different disciplines: visual, technical, business, writing, photography, videography and your industry expertise. While I care about all those things when working with my clients, my most important vetting tool is the business' story. Tell your business' compelling story, highlighting your Unique Selling Proposition and the business' value to your target audience, and all the other pieces of the Web design balancing act do not become slightly less important. In everything you're doing on your website, via Social Media, through Local Search, and on Mobile Media what matters most, even though every creative professional will hate me for saying it, is the story that only you can tell me about *why your business*. This perspective has function trump form every time.

Host Your Own

At the end of reviewing this, I'll tell you that I think you should attempt to build your first website (if you do not yet have one) by yourself, or use a do-it-yourself third-party service, like Google Sites. Why? It is about the education process of how the Web operates. You will get to intimately know what and where HTML and CSS and keywords connect and display in your Web presence, and that can only be helpful. So, you put in about a dozen or so hours and you might not like what you see. Well, then you seek out hiring a Web designer, but at least you know now what the content and structure of the site is that you felt was a good starting place. Your

Web designer will have an idea about where you're coming from and can take you to the next level, if she or he is competent to get you there.

No matter what you do on the Web, I want you to control your brand and therefore always remember to host it yourself if you can.

Additional Reading

• "Does Your Website or Online App Target Kids? Stricter COPPA Rules Go into Effect Soon"
[http://www.sba.gov/community/blogs/community-blogs/business-law-advisor/does-your-website-or-online-app-target-kids-str]

Chapter 4: Plan. Perform. Polish.

> "In preparing for battle I have always found that plans are useless, but planning is indispensable."
>
> ~Dwight D. Eisenhower

P.I.M. ≠ Personal Information Manager. P.I.M. = Plan. Implement. Maintain.

No matter how you do your project planning, planning is the key to making Social Media strategies a success. You can use S.M.A.R.T. goals for your Social Media-enabled business, but do not forget the three parts of any good system: plan, implement and maintain (which includes evaluation). Most people neglect the final step, which is "how do you intend on maintaining your system?" If you do not think about your goals and keep the long-term perspective in mind, you will lose energy and fail to keep the momentum alive that is important for successful strategies to take hold in the social networking and media world.

The Tools (What tools to use to manage your Web, blog, Social Media and more)

There are a dizzying number of software on the market to help you with Social Media and almost everything about online marketing. Here are the tools I recommend and why you should use them:

• Google Analytics [http://google.com/analytics]– (free version) Web traffic data tracking tool that analyzes and synthesizes all this data it collects from Social Media, your website, online advertising, email campaigns and more so that you can make more informed business and marketing decisions.

• HootSuite [http://hootsuite.com],

Tweetdeck [http://tweetdeck.com], Buffer
[http://bufferapp.com], and Argyle Social
[http://argylesocial.com] – If you're trying to
manage and schedule Social Media profiles,
HootSuite and Tweetdeck (owned by Twitter)
provide you the ability to see the major social
networking sites, track Social Media
conversations, collect Web traffic data when
people click on links within your posts, search
for keywords and questions across Social
Media, and schedule posts so that you can set
them at once and then not have to sit there
and wait for 9am to post this tweet and 4pm
to post that Facebook message and so on. If
you'd like to schedule Social Media posts in a
staggered manner so that you're posting at
different times of the day to capture different
audiences when they're on, Buffer provides a
great service. For B2B Social Media, Argyle
Social has you covered, so you should check
them out if you're selling business-to-business.
There are so many more Social Media
management tools, I am actually going to
create a master comparison resource over the

next couple of months, but these few should manage your needs pretty well.

Tip: Because I'm recommending a tool that aggregates your Social Media into one management environment does not mean that you should not visit your own Social Media profiles and outlets on a regular basis. You will find mistakes, changes in the interface and new functionality that you may find **very** useful when you visit these Social Media sites directly on occasion.

- iContact [http://icontact.com], ConstantContact [http://constantcontact.com], AWeber [http://aweber.com], Vertical Response [http://verticalresponse.com] and MailChimp [http://mailchimp.com] – Email marketing and management software is really important for being able to effectively manage messages to your target audience as you collect them over time and through your Web presence marketing. (Note: you should have a strategy in place for capturing email addresses. I'll discuss this in Chapter 9.)

- SugarCRM [http://sugarcrm.org] – Customer Relationship Management (CRM) is a vital way of providing your sales team with the support needed to keep cash flowing, and to help keep customers happy from initial contact to contract, and from fulfillment of your product/service to maintenance of your relationship long-term. SugarCRM is a commercial open source product that I highly recommend for Small Business to take advantage of this amazing technology.

- Wordpress [http://wordpress.org] – the definitive Small Business standard for website and blog development; there are many great services to host your blog and/or website, but I prefer the power that *self-hosting* WordPress provides my clients and my businesses.

Many of these applications about which I write have smartphone software applications (called "apps") that you can use while you are away from your desktop computer or laptop.

Additional reading

- Wikipedia's article on S.M.A.R.T. Goals [http://en.wikipedia.org/wiki/SMART_criteria]

- A great book on productivity and planning: *Getting Things Done* by David Allen [http://w.w3cinc.com/f3ObTv]

Challenge

Write a one-page Social Media marketing plan for the next 12 months. Contact W3 Consulting and request a copy of the One-Page Social Media Marketing Plan template: http://www.w3cinc.com/contact to create your own one-page Social Media marketing plan today. Really, it does not take that long to complete a one-page plan and it's as indispensable as President Eisenhower claims.

Part II - Social Media Success

Chapter 5: Social Rules of Engagement

"Social media is not about the exploitation of technology but service to community."

~Simon Mainwaring

Share = good. Sell = bad.

In business, sales are great. However, social networking and social media are intrinsically "social" not sales. If you are genuine about your long-term investment in the concept of Social Media (producing useful, thought-provoking content and engaging contacts in conversation about that content), you will shine and prosper. If you are fake and just posting sales-y content on the Web in social networking and media platforms, people will ignore you and it will hurt your professional image and company's brand. Social Media can produce tremendous value and sales, but you have to play by the content marketing rules. And, sales happen when your target audience asks, not when you think it should.

A.B.C., Part I = Always be creating.

There are always opportunities for you to be creating content. Everything you do in your business can be captured and used in some way to create content (internally or externally) for your blog, website, podcast, YouTube channel, Pinterest boards, or elsewhere. Note that you must think about great content in all varieties of media (i.e., text, images, links, audio, and video) to provide to your target audience. Content on the World Wide Web (a/k/a the Web, Interwebs, W3, and so on) comes in many formats: text, images/photography, audio and video. (There's a fifth format called "interactive media" which covers games and other kind of digital media that requires a developer to create a program and you develop a contest around the playing of this program.) All of which can be static or dynamic content. Think creatively about your company's goals, how you want to engage your target audience (thinking about their emotional reaction), and then tailor your content to the format.

Tools to Discover

- http://podcastalley.com/

- http://www.businessweek.com/search/podcasting.htm

- http://podbean.com

- http://blogtalkradio.com

- http://images.google.com (Advanced Search)

- http://youtube.com

- http://vimeo.com

- http://mashable.com/2008/02/21/screenc asting-video-tutorials/

Challenge 1

Try to add one type of non-text content (picture, audio or video) to your next posting in your Social Media. (Note: this does not mean you must have created the content. You can post (giving appropriate credit with your own commentary on) content created by someone else.)

A.B.C., Part II = Always be commenting.

The Social Web is about socializing--it's a conversation! Commenting on other people's blogs, message boards, on-line profiles and other "social content" is an easy way to dabble in Social Web without any infrastructure investment. Find industry-related message boards, blogs, social networks/communities, and news sites (most of which now have commenting abilities) and post your opinions and related resources. Challenge or praise (tactfully) incites a good conversation. You get professional exposure, our target audience engages with you from a new perspective (while defining yourself as a "thought leader" or "industry expert"), and

the author gets more Web traffic. Win-win-
win!

Challenge 2

Find your favorite industry-related news or
organization's website and see if they have a
blog, message board, or on-line community,
and plan on commenting on at least three
articles/posts this month.

Continuing Your Twitter Engagement

Once you have a Twitter account, search for
great content to "RT" (re-tweet) and "@" reply
to great tweets on a regular basis. Create a
"comment signature" to promote your Social
Web digital identity in all of your social
profiles. (NOTE: Do not use comment
signatures if the blog/website gives you the
ability to create a profile. People will find
your blog/website via your profile if they find
your comments valuable; comment signatures
are looked as poor taste if the site provides
profiles. It's just part of the Internet culture
that has developed.) As well, talk to your

Web/graphic designer about creating an "avatar" for your company's Web Presence.

* http://gravatar.com

A.B.C., Part III = Always be connecting.

Constantly and consistently grow your on-line social network. Building on the principle behind #4's "Maintain," you must be increasing the number of people you are exposed to, or you become stagnant and your social network will notice and start ignoring you. In some cases, that means out with some of the old before in with anyone new. You can only really engage with about 200-250 people or brands at any given time. Choose them wisely.

Challenge 3

Be cautious about allowing anyone into your social network. You want to grow it, but you want to grow it strategically. If you are marketing to Millennials with expendable income, try not to connect to Baby Boomers. Also, remember the adage: you are what you eat. In Social Networking, the corollary is: you become with whom you associate. And, also: you get what you give.

Limit your time on-line for effectiveness.

Parkinson's Law states that "work expands so as to fill the time available for its completion." If you do not control your time on the Social Web, it will easily start to control you; your whole day can be consumed by social networking and social media content generation. You still need to manage the rest of your business! Social Media marketing and advertising should not and cannot be your only marketing strategy; it's a component. So, make sure to dedicate how much time you need to be effective on-line and put it in your calendar. For example, in the beginning, log into your social networking site(s) once a week on Monday morning for half-hour and try that for a month. You can increase or decrease the time you need to be effective and efficient with your strategies on a monthly basis. You may learn that half-hour daily is necessary, or that half-hour once a week is just as effective. For most Small Business owners who are seeing really great benefits from Social Media, they are usually contributing an average of 1-2 hours daily to content creation, commenting, curating and connecting.

Think like a tech geek.

Okay, at my consultancy, W3 Consulting, we're all tech geeks, so it's easy for me to say that you should think like a techie. However, you will not succeed in Social Media marketing (nay, business!) if you do not take calculated risk. You're an entrepreneur or at least have an entrepreneurial spirit, otherwise you would not be taking the initiative to read this book. (By the way, reward yourself for taking the first step in your road to SoLoMo success!) Tech geeks learn because they are not afraid to "play around" with technology. They will sit with a piece of software or on a website and try out every feature to see what they do. The likelihood is that whatever you are doing is reversible, withstanding common sense (e.g., do not press DELETE if there's no UNDO button). This bravado helps you stumble upon (by the way, check out www.stumbleupon.com!) features, tricks and shortcuts, and new Web services you would not otherwise.

Chapter 6: Social Media Enhances IN REAL LIFE (IRL) Activities

"Communication leads to community,
that is, to understanding, intimacy
and mutual valuing."
~Rollo May

Although Social Media might have spurred a revolution, it was not meant to create a virtual existence for the human race. Dynamically, collectively Web users (and developers) felt the interactivity on the Internet was limiting. We were, and continue to be, spending more and more time online because it is where so much of our day-to-day functionality has migrated; exploring, shopping, learning, earning a living, and communicating with colleagues, clients, friends and family long distances away from us all happen by and large facilitated by the Web. So, the Social Web developed new tools to help connect us better. In this chapter, I am going to give you an extensive list with brief explanations of each of the major social technologies, along with their potential applications in a Small Business environment.

It is important to recognize that social technologies were not meant to replace our interactivity with real people, in real life. "IRL" is a popular acronym among Millennials and younger, proving that younger generations are feeling *something* about the segmentation of their online and offline life; although, I am not sure what that something is and the average Millennial probably could not articulate the feeling. I will draw the line in the sand *in a business perspective* for any of these social technologies that I am going to outline here, though. If you engage in the Social Web purely for it to stay on the Social Web, you are doing it wrong. Period. Social technologies (Social Media, social networking, and everything about being a "Social

Business") must enhance your consumers' lives offline, or IRL activities. You must always remember that there are human beings on the other side of your computers, tablets and mobile phones when you are writing, recording and interacting with social content. If your activities, content and responses are not enhancing their **real** lives you are missing the boat and you are contributing to the vapid "chatter" and Old Way thinking that will eat away at your brand's value (and ultimately your business' longevity), as well as your consumer's enjoyment of your product or service. The solution: think about how your consumer's life is better when you implement any of the social technologies to follow. There are many ways to make these social tools do so. Be creative. Be open. Be active. And, most of all, be **real**.

Social applications, applied

Here's a non-definitive but, I believe, good sampling of social software with possible business uses. I hope this helps unlock some creative ideas for ways your business can engage using the Social Web.

Blogging

I cover blogging, podcasting and vlogging extensively in Chapter 9, so head over there for that discussion.

Clipping

If you have ever clipped a newspaper or magazine article and handed it to a family member or friend, that's what Clipping is on the Social Web. Evernote [http://evernote.com] is just such a reference tool. You can selectively share notebooks with exclusive customers, email customers weekly or monthly note/notebook links to articles or other information that you have collected from the Web that might be useful to them. Clipping is a great "touchpoint" tool for sharing information with your audience.

Instant messaging

Instant messaging, or IM, is a synchronous (real-time) text, audio and/or video conversation tool provided by many different services (mostly free), including AOL Chat, Apple iChat / FaceTime, Google Hangouts, Yahoo! Messenger, MSN/Live Messenger, Skype (owned by Microsoft), and many others. While it is no matter to me the flavor of IM that you choose, you should select the platform where most of your customers are active. Instant messaging can be an amazing customer service tool, with some of them allowing you to embed the chat functionality on your website and handle customer service and initial sales questions directly from Web visitors to your site. Video instant messaging (in the form of Skype and Google+ Hangouts) gives you the ability to deliver services "face-to-face" virtually with your target audience, give sales presentations, give Web-based seminars, demonstrate your product, and conduct focus groups for marketing research. One burgeoning growth area is the use of Google+ Hangouts on Air, which is the idea of video instant messaging with up to nine other people (with as many others watching and contributing via text-based conversation within the Hangout). So to be clear, you are able to have up to 10 total people in a virtual "chat room" with as many people watching, plus this whole session can be recorded and published to your YouTube account if you want. Not only does this mean you can do panel discussions of experts, meet with several customers at a time to discuss product development, and bring in multiple staff members to help customers understand your product, **but** you can also get great content to publish to your YouTube channel and syndicate to your Social Media channels!

Internet forums

The discussion boards on the World Wide

Web are not dead, as some may like to think! In many communities, the most vibrant social interactions happen via Web boards that communicate either exclusively by discussions happening on a specific web page with different discussions segmented by topic (i.e., "discussion threads"), or via email where the conversations happen by sending email messages back and forth with forum participants. The posts are not only emailed to the others but also get posted to the Web board. Some of these tools I would recommend include Google Groups, Yahoo! Groups, and User Voice. While some more techie folks will argue with me over what constitutes an email list-serve, an Internet forum, an online bulletin board and such (and that it is Web 1.0 software that does not even belong categorized as Social Media), but because the social technologies are so blended today I will take the criticism and let you decide whether to use it or not based on its usefulness in your business. The way you will use such technology is usually as a Frequently

Asked Questions (FAQ) repository (which can be great for search engine traffic!) where your customers can ask and your staff can answer questions so that when potential and past customers visit your website they can get answers without having to call you every five minutes on how to use or fix your product. Additionally, these discussions usually open up new opportunities through the dialog of new features, missing elements from your service lines, and your customers cluing you into new markets they might like to see you differentiate your product or service. While some may say the Internet forum is a dying breed, I think they are just hidden gems because many are behind security for exclusivity. They are alive and well!

eLearning

Very similar to Google+ Hangouts, eLearning tools are similar to physical classrooms except they allow you to teach or conduct services in a virtual learning environment. You have the ability to be live or record yourself on camera, show a presentation slide-deck/visuals, share documents, receive files, and manage a discussion among the students (if you'd like). Some examples are Udemy, BigBlueButton (with Matterhorn), and CourseSites (by Blackboard). While you may think only teachers and professors at academic institutions would want to use these, think of the possibilities of hosting full courses of your business' educational programs within a secure environment (and in the case of Udemy, handling payment and having a ready marketplace of learners). These can be on-demand so you can be sleeping while people are taking your courses...and you're making money! You can use this for staff training, client demos and training, providing coaching and consulting to many people, all remotely (so you can deliver services around the globe to people in different locations from your home or office).

- http://udemy.com

- http://bigbluebutton.org

- http://coursesites.com

Massively multiplayer online games

MMOGs (the acronym for "massively multiplayer online games") are games that allow you to play with people from wherever they're connected to the Internet in the same simulation environment. The US Armed Forces uses these games to train troops about what live combat feels like before they're actually deployed. If your business has any connection to health/fitness, speech/language skills, any kind of games or entertainment, these are fantastic opportunities to get creative about sponsoring players in the MMOGs to get brand recognition, but also to become a part of these communities and sell your products/services. These games can be Web browser-based, console-based (like Microsoft XBox, Sony Playstation, Nintendo Wii, and others), and mobile/smartphone devices. They include some of these categories: exploration, FPS (first-person shooter), flight simulation, role-playing games (RPGs), social games, and real-time strategy. Get your innovative juices flowing and think of ways in which you can engage your customers to play against each other for recognition by your company and prizes.

Media sharing

From photos to videos to eBooks, we should really call the Social Media Revolution the Media Sharing Revolution! Media sharing is just what it sounds like; they're sites where you can upload and share, discuss and get recognition for the content your producing. From the world's largest video search engine, YouTube, to Flickr (one of the largest photography sharing websites) to Lafango (a site for talent and talent seekers based out of the New York Metropolitan area), people are filling their profiles and pages with amazing content. Where might your business see opportunities? One, you can find great content to share with your audience in these media sharing sites. Also, think about the opportunity to create and share your business' story through video, photos and more in these distribution platforms (where appropriate). And, finally, you can build communities on these platforms if many or most of your target audience are active there. Do you run a dance school, martial arts studio, health/fitness club/gym/personal training practice, or any kind of physical health & wellness service? Well, you should look into YouTube, Vimeo, Blip.tv, Tout, and Lafango for showcasing your talent, your customers' talents and progress, and encouraging folks who may be on the fence about getting involved. In the case of the photo-sharing site, SmugMug, you're able to set up a site where you charge for people to buy and use your photos, so if you're a photographer that might be a great revenue source if you're shooting stock photography.

- http://youtube.com

- http://flickr.com

- http://vimeo.com

- http://lafango.com

- http://blip.tv

- http://tout.com

- http://smugmug.com

Media cataloging

Also known as social cataloging applications, media cataloging is the concept of taking your entertainment and organizing it digitally and mostly publicly so that you can share and discuss them. While these can be accomplished in Clipping applications as discussed above, these are ready-made communities of media enthusiasts. If you're an avid book reader, audiophile, or movie buff, you can connect with your audience where your industry, entertainment and your business intersect. If you are the industry expert or thought leader, this is an opportunity to compile and share your thoughts on the material that's out there in your field. For example, are there really only 10 good books that cover your profession? Well, now is your opportunity to tell your target audience why, or why they should not, read one particular book over another. These public advertisements establish credibility and authority for you as the subject matter expert.

- http://goodreads.com

- http://shelfari.com

- http://spotify.com

- http://pandora.com

- http://jango.com

- http://songza.com

- http://librarything.com

- http://last.fm

- http://flixster.com /
http://rottentomatoes.com

- http://imdb.com

Online dating

While this may seem to have limited usefulness, online dating is a huge industry and has many opportunities for the Social Media-savvy business owner. There are more than 102 million singles over the age of 18 years in the United States as of the last census, which is approximately one-third of our population! Don't ignore your customers! Online dating websites are social at their core, trying to help you find a spouse. For businesses trying to get marketing exposure, there are advertising opportunities galore, especially if you're a licensed clinical therapist, relationship counselor or matchmaker. You may also want to create an actual profile and engage directly with folks who need your business service or product (if there is an ability to do so appropriately, noting that you are a professional/business).

Social bookmarking

Social bookmarking is a content curators' paradise; or, a digital hoarders' limitless storage attic.

For a business, it is amazingly an untapped opportunity for website traffic! If you create great content and share it in social bookmarking sites, you give your followers an opportunity to create many more inbound links to your website through the sharing capabilities within these sites. As well, by adding these elements to your website (like AddThis and Shareaholic), you are empowering your Web visitors to share your content into social bookmarking sites as well as their personal social networks!

- http://getpocket.com

- http://delicious.com

- http://digg.com

- http://reddit.com

- http://diigo.com

- http://instapaper.com

- http://readability.com

Social login

When you want to join a website or service, you typically need to add your personal information to their Web database engine. If you do not know the developers or company producing the website or service it can feel precarious to give your personal, private information to a stranger. Enter Social Login. This is feature uses your Facebook, Google, Google+, Twitter or other social networks' login credentials to identify you and sign you up for the service, thereby protecting your data from a website or service while still being able to use it. As well, who needs to remember another password, right? If you want to increase the number of people who sign up on your blog or website for gaining access to selected or premium content, social login is the way to increasing sign-ups.

- http://livefyre.com

- http://disqus.com

- Facebook Connect: http://developers.facebook.com/docs/guides/web/

- Twitter Connect: https://dev.twitter.com/docs/auth/sign-twitter

- Google OAuth 2.0: https://developers.google.com/accounts/docs/OAuth2

- Google+ Sign-in: https://developers.google.com/+/

Social networks

By now you probably know what a social network is, but it's basically a website that enables users to communicate around a specific or general interest. Businesses can actually create their own social networks on their own website or by using different services that serve as an out-the-box social networking platform.

• http://ning.com

• http://socialgo.com

• http://buddypress.org

Wikis

Wikis are like living magazines on the Web that are usually open for everyone (or, anyone) to edit. Wikipedia is the most prevalent example of a wiki. While this may seem daunting for Small Business, wikis are really easily manageable and can serve as a working manual for customers in your industry to which you, your staff, your vendors, partners, colleagues and customers can all contribute. It can serve as a major pull of Search Engine traffic. Never fear if you want a little more control; check out Tiki Wiki for more enterprise controls for limiting who can access and edit your wiki so you can make parts only viewable and editable internally and other parts open and accessible to your target audience.

- http://mediawiki.org

- http://info.tiki.org/tiki-index.php

Creating Your Own Social Media Platform

While this book is not designed to launch your own Social Media platform for monetizing or your business, you should know that just like the list of *Social networks* section above, there is software available for you to put a platform together for each of

these (and many other categories of Social Media) on your own website. If it behooves your business to build traffic by building a platform for your target audience to commune on your website and put content on it (text-based, video, audio, photography, and more) then you may want to look at the options of free social software for your website available
[http://en.wikipedia.org/wiki/List_of_free_sof tware_for_Web_2.0_Services]. This is **not** for the faint of heart but hosting a social platform on your website can be quite lucrative for Web traffic building and if it serves your business in bringing sales.

Chapter 7: Social Media Is a Component of Marketing, Not Vice Versa

"Stop selling. Start helping."
~Zig Ziglar

I visualize Small Business Marketing as a pie with five equal parts: sales, referral networking, advertising, public relations, and branding/corporate identity.

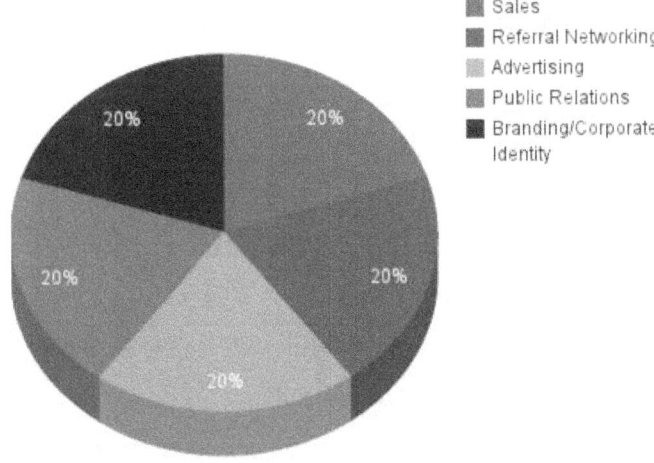

The Marketing Mix (The 4 P's and 4C's of Marketing)

Traditional marketing education teaches you that your major marketing management decisions can be classified in one of the following four categories:

• Product

• Price

• Place (distribution)

• Promotion

These variables are known as the marketing mix or the 4 P's of marketing. They are the variables that marketing managers can control in order to best satisfy customers in the target market.

The business attempts to generate a positive response in the target market by blending these four marketing mix variables in an optimal manner.

Product

The product is the physical product or service

offered to the consumer. In the case of physical products, it also refers to any services or conveniences that are part of the offering. Product decisions include aspects such as function, appearance, packaging, service, warranty, etc.

Price

Pricing decisions should take into account profit margins and the probable pricing response of competitors. Pricing includes not only the list price, but also discounts, financing, and other options such as leasing.

Place

Place (or placement) decisions are those associated with channels of distribution that serve as the means for getting the product to the target customers. The distribution system performs transactional, logistical, and facilitating functions. Distribution decisions include market coverage, channel member selection, logistics, and levels of service.

Promotion

Promotion decisions are those related to communicating and selling to potential consumers. Since these costs can be large in proportion to the product price, a break-even analysis should be performed when making promotion decisions. It is useful to know the value of a customer in order to determine whether additional customers are worth the cost of acquiring them. Promotion decisions involve advertising, public relations, media types, etc.

However, in recent years, a new paradigm has shifted toward a more consumer-focused categorization, called the 4C's: *Consumer* (what are the needs/wants from your consumer's perspective?); *Cost* (how much will this product/service mean in total cost of ownership to the consumer, factoring in maintenance and upgrades over time?), *Communications* (How are you providing and receiving information to/from your consumer before, during and after the sale?); and,

Convenience (How easy it for your consumer to search for, learn about and purchase your service/produce?). Below I've taken the five equal parts of Small Business Marketing and married them with the 4C's via my recommendations for making a marketing impact on your bottom line.

Marketing Recommendations

1.   Marketing metrics and evaluation are so important to the success of your business. If you focus on positive outcomes you are far more likely to succeed at them since you are guaranteed to fail if you focus on negative outcomes or do not focus at all, so pay attention to the positive trends in your numbers and grow with them.

2.   Balance your marketing efforts across all parts of marketing; sales, advertising, public relations, referral networking, and corporate branding/identity, as the above pie chart shows. Local Search, Social Media, and Mobile Media are remarkably aspects of each

of these slices of your Marketing Pie.

Sales

1.   An ancient Chinese proverb teaches that "A cheap price is a shortcut to being cheated." I want you to uphold an excellent reputation among your clientele and maintain the highest standards for your clients' desires. This assures your clients that any encounter with them will make them feel that every cent of your fee was well-invested. Assess your fees and make sure that they stand in line with industry standards; as a general rule of thumb, your prices are too low.

2.   **Outline your sales process.** | Sales is a numbers game. You need to create

controls and follow a methodology. Find the weaknesses in your methodology through tracking your efforts and then minimize those weaknesses until your sales methods are solid.

3. **Sales happen on the World Wide Web on your website.** | I know there are fancy tools that allow you set up eCommerce (online shopping) tools on your Facebook Page and so forth, but I'm sorry, by and large no one ever goes to your Facebook Page after they "Like" the page so your fancy Facebook Page shop is useless. Again, Sales happen on your website. Don't direct your hard-earned traffic away from your website to Social Media with Facebook, Twitter and Pinterest icons. Use social plugins to keep them on

your website! I'll say it again, sales happen on your website.

Advertising

Video did NOT kill the radio star!
Traditional and new media should be utilized in balance. Period. So many people are forgetting traditional media outlets (print, television, radio, direct mail, and other analog advertising) in their overall advertising budget and strategic planning. If you tried advertising in the past and it "didn't work," I mean no offense by this but you probably did it wrong. You need to make sure you select the right publications, at the right time and using the right ad visuals and copy, as well as advertising for an extended period of time so that your advertisements build up in the minds of your buyer. If you do not have the budget for it, you do not have the budget for it and it's fine. It's just plain

false that offline advertising does not work.

On the flip side, if you do have a slim budget, you may want to try your hands at using online advertising. There are so many options but look into Google AdWords, LinkedIn Ads (if you are B2B), Twitter Ads, Facebook Ads, and more. If you really want to make an impact find and make direct relationships with local websites and blogs where your target audience visits often, and make deals to advertise on those websites. You may pay more money per ad than you would with the above major ad networks, but the click-throughs from those sites may be so much more effective because you *know* your audience that are visiting those local websites and blogs.

Public Relations

Get testimonials from as many

customers as possible and syndicate those testimonials at every level of marketing (including Social Media), especially in your Marketing Collateral.

For example, have every client that writes a testimonial in provided feedback forms/surveys or on a predetermined Social Media site(s) get a substantial discount on their next month's service. You cannot pay enough for this positive publicity.

A strategy that is very powerful is to ask them to recommend you on your LinkedIn profile, and also to have clients recommend specific products/services on your LinkedIn company profile (the one you'll create in Chapter 13). Now the testimonials are cross-pollinated to everyone perusing your LinkedIn profile and company page through LinkedIn's search and browsing functionality, and you can easily copy those testimonials to your website and offline marketing collateral.

Referral Networking

1.   Every person in your organization that is empowered to handle sales & marketing for your company should strive to attend four referral networking events per month. Build a referral network marketing plan and be diligent about creating a centralized database of relationships. This may require a customer relationship management (CRM) system such as SalesForce.com, or better try the open-source CRM, SugarCRM, which I mentioned in Chapter 4.

2.   Create a written referral network marketing plan which incorporates the creation of a

database (which is basically what a customer relationship management ("CRM") system is).

3.   The general rule of referral networking is to have some communication with your best referrers of business every 20 days.

4.   Ask your clients for referrals on a regular basis.

5.   Thank people well for giving you referrals. If you can and where appropriate, thank them publicly via Social Media. People love the gratitude, affirmation and recognition, and therefore it stimulates them to send you more referrals.

Chapter 8: Social Media Is Not a Popularity Contest

"It's much easier on the emotions when one sees life as an experiment rather than a struggle for popularity."

~Criss Jami

In almost every high school growing up, there seemed to be (and still are, I imagine) cliques. I remember there were the preppies, the skaters, the cheerleaders, the stoners, the hippies, the jocks, the goths, the grunge crowd, the nerds, the band/choir members, and the thespians. You name it, and students found a way to categorize and define themselves into groups where they felt comfortable. For some it was merely a defensive maneuver, like gazelles grazing together on the Sahara Desert plains and hoping the cheetah or monitor lizard hunting that day nabs one of the weaker. While for others it was a sign of their economic or social class in their high school community. Some people have never outgrown their high school categorization, and some have long-forgotten they were a part of one until they go to class reunions and the hierarchy magically reappear like no one ever left. People naturally self-organize in the absence of someone creating groups from a top-down approach. I say this all to suggest that you should attempt to influence your business' brand as best as you can by watching your target audience group naturally (just like high school cliques) and then communicating to these groups in simple, effective messages via Social Media.

As I discussed in Chapter 1, humans like to gather and there's a comfortable number of people to make a conversation. Your business needs to do some research to figure out how many of those people need to be around talking regularly to make it a good conversation. However, the rampant hoarding of followers and fans via Social Media is a misguided pathway to SoLoMo success. The best Social Media metric for the startup or veteran business owner is *influence*, not the numbers of followers she has. Influence is the call-to-action ratio of your business' communications. If I ask you to do something, how likely are you to do it? What's the motivation (intrinsically and extrinsically) for you to do what I ask? If you can determine that for each of your audiences, you're on the road to success. Numbers are a past tense metric, in my eyes, when it comes to Social Media conversations. They represent a conversation you had with a number of people, and only a potential for future eyeballs seeing your content. I want to see you influencing your audience and when they say, "How high?" when you say, "Jump!" then you're doing the right things in Social Media.

We've learned from social scientists that when you group people together, the larger the group gets the less influence you have over the individuals in the group. Here's what I do not want to see for you: you have 10,000 likes on your Facebook Page, 6,000 Twitter followers, and 5,000 repins on Pinterest; however, every time you post with a call-to-action you get tons of likes, hearts and comments and **negligible or no visits to your website**. That's the worst kind of influence...because there is none! You're running a business not a charity. (And, if you're actually running a charity, my advice still applies. I'm not going to stand idly by if people are not doing *real* things in *real* life when you ask.) If you have 50 followers and most of them clamor to do what you command, that's the kind of influence I want to see your business have. Perhaps that's all you will ever need in terms of active participants in the conversations to have a wildly thriving business. It's possible that you'll need a few hundred or even a few thousand active participants in the conversation to make it worth your while. Do your research and do not count numbers for counting sake.

At the end of the day, I use numbers of fans or followers on Social Media as ways to motivate my clients to get to milestones with content and engagement. It helps to celebrate when you hit your first 100 followers, next 250, and 500 and so on! It's fun! But, more importantly, I want you to pay attention to the people who act when you ask. What did you say? What did you ask them to do? And, how much did they share your call-to-action?

Chapter 9: Your Blog Is Your Social Media Headquarters

> "...[Blogs] are far superior to corporate Web sites, Facebook pages, and Twitter accounts with regard to inbound marketing. If your social media objective is even tangentially about attracting new customers, the SEO value of the blog alone makes it a suitable hub."
>
> ~Jay Baer

Start a Blog.

Every Small Business owner should start a blog that you host on your own website. Not only does this act as your communications headquarters for your business, it's your Web property not someone else's asset (e.g., Facebook, Google, Twitter, LinkedIn or another social media service).

We find that successful, small business bloggers utilize the power of their blogs by good preparation, have planned posts anchor their blog presence, and create a brand impact consistent with all of their marketing efforts. First, good preparation consists of using a blogging platform (software) that you are comfortable with and that's installed properly. We generally recommend that if you are serious about becoming a small business blogger you decide on an editorial calendar with publishing dates, mission statement for your blog (that is not just about your business specifically), and to write at least five to eight weeks of content for your blog before launching (which allows you to take vacations, time off and put out fires without blog inconsistency). We recommend WordPress as the small business blogger's platform of choice; we usually recommend registering a domain specifically branded for your blog (www.yourblogname.com) and hosting your own WordPress blog (which you can register your domain and host your WordPress blog with your current Web host, or if they do not provide these services you can find many domain registrars to suit your business' needs). Most of our clients use Google Calendar as their blog's editorial calendar, since it's easily accessible (desktop, Web and mobile) and collaborative. And, while you may initially plan posting about weekly on your blog, that does not mean you do not blog when a truly beneficial thought comes to mind that you'd like to share with your target audience. These are known as unplanned posts and it can be as simple as a picture/infographic/video that you want to share or make commentary on to your blog readers, or it can be a well-written paragraph or two of your thoughts. Finally, our experience with our blogging clients has shown that making sure your planned blog posts are in line with the rest of your marketing is vital to long-term impact. For example, if you have a retail gift shop, blog posts should cover topics related to your marketing (print advertising, media advertising, publicity and so on) for upcoming holidays throughout the calendar year. We wish you the best of luck in your endeavor to be a successful small business blogger, and make sure to send us a link [http://w3cinc.com/contact/] to it once it's up and running so we can subscribe to the blog feed.

Do not think too much about the technology that runs the Social Web (sometimes called Web 2.0, and most often called Social Media and/or Social Networking) engine. There are many sites that do the technical work for you (see the links below) and leave you to just think about the generation of great content. Your duty as a small business blogger is to write great content, which means that you need to enlist the tools you learned in high school English class: define and know your audience, outline your blog entries (summary/statement of purpose, introduction, body and summary), and proofread for spelling, style (casual, active voice is best), mood (i.e., tense) consistency, and other grammatical issues. Also, note that blogging for business marketing purposes should give information/resources, should be clear and succinct (300-600 words) and call your target audience to action (what do you want them to do?). If you could speak directly to your customers and potential buyers of your product/service every day, week or month, what would you say? Finally, and as I said earlier because it's worth repeating, create an editorial calendar. The publishing industry (books, magazines, newspapers, websites and other periodicals) all have editorial calendars (sometimes outlining their topics a year in advance)--you *must* too.

I'm going to repeat myself from Chapter 3, but it warrants repetition: host your own where you can and are able. Your blog is the most important component of your Social Web presence; do not leave it necessarily in someone else's hands completely. The key component is that you control the hosted domain or URLs (or the service you're using can redirect it elsewhere later), and that you can control the content should you want to move it somewhere else at a subsequent time.

• http://www.wordpress.org (self-hosted version only; recommended again for its rich features/plugins and portability over the premium service at WordPress.com)

• www.blogger.com (Google-owned, simple to use)

• www.tumblr.com (fairly new but worthwhile blog service, now owned by Yahoo!)

Beyond Beginner Blogging

Once you get yourself into a regular blogging schedule (3-5 weeks of steady posts, talk to your Web designer/programmer about installing a blog on your company's website (e.g., www.your-domain.com/blog), or getting a separate domain for your blog (e.g., www.yourblogsname.com or www.yourblogsname.blog). You can then move your content from your current blog site and move it to your new blog. (Why give your earned Web traffic to another website?) Have your Web designer/programmer make sure to install software to monitor your Web traffic, such as Google Analytics (it's a free, robust product that will suit you most businesses well). Your Web host may already be tracking and reporting this data to you, but you have to find out where they are publishing it for you in your Web hosting dashboard (or, sometimes called "control panel" or "cPanel").

•   Shameless Plug: W3C Web Services has reliable and affordable domain registration services, and WordPress blog hosting [http://w.w3cinc.com/oX3nsz]

Small Business Blogging Versus Being a Bloggerpreneur

A word of warning: while it is tempting to put online advertisements on your small business website, I recommend against it as a general rule. You provide a product/service, which you want your target audience to buy. Do not distract them from buying your product/service by putting very low-paying online display/text advertisements on your website. There are a few circumstances where you might use affiliate ads on your website; W3 Consulting does on our website, for example, because we absolutely love the two or three software tools we promote there...it is really not for the money! If you're a Bloggerpreneur it's a different story because you have to monetize your website to make money, most likely. Small business websites do not monetize their websites, they want to market their business' products and services through their websites!

The Ultimate Small Business Website/Blog Strategy

There is a well-known (by Web professionals) and so extremely powerful but frequently unused methodology (by most small businesses) that can drive great amounts of Web traffic and increase sales. I commonly call it the "Digital Download" methodology. First, create immensely-valued information packages (digital media, primarily). This is truly the most difficult challenge of this website/blog strategy. Next, go to Social Media and listen for conversations about needs for this immensely valuable information and direct people to it. Of course this information lives on your website or blog behind an email signup form. (This is something easy enough for your Web developer to help you implement.) In order for them to get this information they highly value, they must give you their name, (optionally) company/organization, phone, budget, demographics, and needs/wants...but most importantly their **email address**. Email marketing is the most powerful digital marketing force online short of SEO, in my humble opinion. You must be collecting and communicating your business' value through your compelling story (remember, Chapter 6's section, *Function Over Form*?) via email to your audience.

A more advanced technique is to create pages on your website or blog that market these digital downloads to Search Engines via keyword searches. People searching find the pages and click on the download links, enter their email addresses and get your content. About a week after they download, you can now reach out to them to answer any questions they had; no sales talk required. These potential clients are usually so happy you were so helpful in educating them, they'll think of you first when they're ready to buy, if they do not do so right there in that email response or a 10-minute phone call.

Challenge

Schedule two to three hours on the next three Mondays in your calendar. The first hour of that time you need to turn off your cellphone, all your mobile devices, your computer's connection to the Internet. Yes, I am asking you to disconnect from the Web; it is just temporary. Pull out some colored pens, crayons or markers and some large sheets of drawing paper. Now, get creative. Map out your customers' greatest challenges, your products' or services' best benefits, and what are the most frequently asked questions about your business or organization. What can you create digitally (i.e., PDF, video, audio or software, even if you are not the technical person creating the item) that would entice your target audience to come to your website—and give you some information about themselves—to download this item?

Chapter 10: Facebook Madness

> "People have told me 'Betty,
> Facebook is a great way to keep in
> touch with old friends...' At my age,
> if I wanted to keep in touch with
> old friends, I'd need a Ouija board."
>
> ~Betty White

Everyone is Facebook-crazy! I call it Facebook Madness. Yes, Facebook is amazing for many reasons. If your business can be related to me as a consumer when I am interacting with my *friends and family* then your business can likely market to me on Facebook very effectively. If you're business-to-business (B2B), you should *likely* skip Facebook and move to Twitter, Google+, a social network that is personal-business neutral, or LinkedIn which is specifically business. Facebook is for my personal life and if your business invades that with discussion about my professional and business life, I am likely to think poorly about you.

Below are the primary areas I recommend that you get started with on Facebook with my caveats noted.

Profiles

The bottom line as to whether you use a Profile or Group for your business' Facebook presence: never. I know that some will relent and give me all the reasons that their particular reasoning for using their Profile or a Group that they have set up for their business is better than setting up a Page. And, some will note that Facebook themselves made Pages as a second-thought for businesses. My hope is that by explaining some key features of Pages and key disadvantages of Groups and Profiles, that you will go ahead and take the effort to launch your business' Facebook Page in the not-too-distant future and then proceed to do away with your other Facebook presences as soon as practicable.

Groups

Facebook Groups are wonderful tools but for small communities within Facebook, such as committees, focus groups, boards, and groups of friends. Although it may be tempting to create a Group because you've heard of the few "advantages" over Pages, we highly dissuade you from thinking this is true. While you can send messages directly to members of groups, member engagement is higher in groups thanks to the generally smaller size, and the discussion thread feature set, Groups are missing the core extensibility of Pages — applications, analytics and Web coding functionality. Over time, Facebook engagement will be completely about the functionality of your Pages as much as they are about the content you provide. You will cut yourself off from the powerful mobile advantages of Facebook marketing that I detail in Part IV – Mobile Marketing Success.

Pages

Facebook Pages are the *de facto* home for businesses and brands on Facebook. Every small business should stake their claim to their Facebook Page (especially if you have a retail location). Facebook Ads and ad networks allow you to direct traffic to Facebook Pages, you can have unlimited fans following your Page, and users associate Pages with companies they like and trust. Every business' marketing needs are different on Facebook, so we will give you what we can that is universally beneficial.

Facebook Pages are indexed by all the major search engines (even though the posts are usually blocked by Facebook from being indexed individually), so make sure that your Info Tab is filled out properly and is keyword-rich. The most highly engaging content on Facebook are pictures, videos, links (to third-party sites or your own website), questions then interactive media (like apps). You can use this information to create a healthy mix of content to drive traffic and engagement.

Next, make use of the Facebook Applications that are available to use for your customers; if you host frequent events, use the Events app, or if you want to give coupons to loyal and/or discount customers, you can create a new Tab that provides a coupon when someone gives you their email address. The utilities are endless.

And, finally, remember that people are on Facebook to do personal, consumer-based activities. They are not thinking about being sold to or about business-to-business activities when they're surfing their Newsfeed and communicating with their Friends. That said, make sure you are tailoring your content to captivate people while they are in a family-and-friends perspective.

Bonus

This is all said in the context that the best

place for you to own/manage your target audience's contacts and other data is not Facebook (or any other social network). Your company's domain and your Web content is owned by you on your website, whereas Facebook has equal rights to your data once you upload it there. If Facebook becomes passé or shuts down or is sold, your data and connections may be lost. You can also get much richer data from your target audience viewing your website than Facebook gives you in their Insights analytics tool, not to mention the ability to create a visually cohesive, branded experience for your audience while viewing your website. Lastly, Facebook has the ultimate control over allowing you to have your Page, or not; they can shut down your Profile, Group or Page without reason. You cannot give anyone that much control over your business.

Facebook is one of the most powerful, pervasive social networking and advertising platforms on the Internet today. However, Facebook has many issues (and many more opportunities!) that you need to know before you involve your business on the platform. Get on Facebook, but consult business and Web, mobile & digital technology strategy consultants on how to engage on Facebook appropriately and effectively.

If nothing else, make sure to read Facebook's Terms of Use. Additionally, use Facebook's Help sections to their fullest extent. Protect your personal and professional brand from Facebook!

- www.facebook.com/terms.php

- http://www.reclaimprivacy.org/

Chapter 11: Start Short: Twitter

"Brevity is the soul of wit."

~William Shakespeare

Create a Twitter Profile

Once you create your Twitter account, Twitter will take you through a process to see what contacts are also on Twitter. (Don't make the mistake of accidentally emailing everyone. The utility should just go through and tell you which contacts are already on Twitter.) Follow as many contacts as you find interesting and follow everyone that requests to follow you in the initial days; you can always stop following them once you get the hang of Twitter. Start tweeting!

• http://twitter.com/w3consulting ← Follow us on Twitter!

Headlines, Headlines, Headlines

I will let you in on a little not-so-secret about Twitter: it's nothing more than writing captivating headlines in a specialized format. I recommend that you walk through your neighborhood grocery store and as you peruse the checkout magazine stands, look at the headlines that you come across. In effect, these are frameworks for tweets you can use in your own business. If you replace your business' keywords with the ones of the magazines you see, you can most often create your own tweets and then start to modify those models to be more and more effective.

The formula is usually something like this:

```
Headline (with #hashtag(s), if
appropriate) plus a hyperlink, plus
#hashtag(s).
```

For example, let's take a make-believe pharmacy's common cold remedy and how I would write a tweet to get people to click on the link:

```
Finally! A #cure for the common
cold! Learn more:
http://t.co/123456 #nasopharyngitis
```

Okay, so first, note that my tweet is really exciting! A cure for the common cold?! Who wouldn't want to learn more about that? As well, I have provided hashtags (here, #cure and #nasopharyngitis, a medical term used for the common cold) for keywords I want Search Engines to start relating to my business. These hashtags start linking those (and related) keywords to my Twitter profile and also to the Web address I have assigned to my profile as well, presumably my business blog or website. I could have also combined common cold to create the hashtag #commoncold but I did not want to overdo it; the term is now in my tweet and together with the hashtags have created a relationship organically in the Twitter Search algorithm.

Finally, you know there is not a cure for the common cold so I do not believe in lying to people; the headline is the hook and acceptable to catch our attention. But, in your blog post or the content you have led people to, you need to then provide the juxtaposition of the tweet with reality. For example, my blog post's first sentence might read, "While there may be no actual cure for the common cold, our cold remedy will make you feel like there is, and here's how!" From there, I would explain how my cold remedy works and provide links within my website to its core benefits.

This is also a good place to note that you can have many tweets to one blog post, which is dissimilar to having many Facebook posts to one blog article. It's one the core reasons why I believe that Twitter can always drive more Web traffic to your website or blog than Facebook, if your target audience is on both social networks. If I wanted to, I could write seven effective tweets for one blog post. I could then tweet one each day at different times for an entire week and capture different traffic from followers and others looking for key terms in tweets. You have multiplied the traffic to your blog sixfold from Twitter by writing these additional tweets. In the initial tweet, you might push out the blog post title itself and then six others that would include more interrogative (question) tweets, and as you will see on the newsstands other headline formats. Use the power of the headline formats you see to create new tweets that work for your business, including:

• How-to ("How to make your #commoncold disappear! http://t.co/123456"),

• Numbers 3 and 7 (things that come in threes and seven (or less) items are easily remembered, and are very appealing to readers; think about why we have US telephone numbers comprised of three-digit area codes and seven-digit local numbers),

• outstanding facts (as high-contrast percentages and shocking statistics stand out), and

• unfinished sentences (so that if you take your interrogative tweets above and write the answer but leave out the direct object, it answers the question when you click on the link; for example, "The key to conquering the #commoncold is... http://t.co/123456").

A great tweet that really hooked me was one in which the business owner wrote a tweet about her business *shutting down*. Shocked, I clicked on the link and learned that she was going *on vacation*; she needed everyone to know who to contact in her absence and effectively got all of our attention to do so!

Advancing on Twitter

Seek out experts in your industry on Twitter and try to engage them in conversation with either direct messages (known as a "DM"; you can only DM someone who already follows you) or @replies. Also, talk to your Web/graphic designer to edit your Twitter profile, background image and profile image to match your company's brand. (You can also try your hand at doing it yourself using the free Twitter tools or Themeleon—look for the link on Twitter or just use Google Search to find it.) Finally, go learn about "tweetchats" and engage in at least one per week in your industry.

• Twitter Chat Schedule [http://goo.gl/BC67M] (there used to be more than 600 chats in the schedule but some ne'er-do-well deleted it; however, the Twitter community is rebuilding the list so check back often for new Twitter chats being added regularly)

• Gnosis Arts has a List of Twitter Tweetchats [http://gnosisarts.com/index.php?title=Tweetc hat_Wiki]

• Twubs.com's Twitter Chat Schedule [http://twubs.com/twitter-chats]

• Twitter Chat Schedule on TweetReports.com [http://tweetreports.com/twitter-chat-schedule/]

Attending Live & Virtual Events

Twitter is a real-time communication platform (even with many other useful purposes for consumer and business brands alike). Hashtags are the vehicle by which you can follow and engage in live event conversations.

There are many Web tools (e.g., http://tweetgrid.com or http://twitterfall.com) and desktop software (e.g., http://tweetdeck.com) that allow you to plug in an event hashtag and then follow along and interact with live and virtual attendees of the event. Another point of importance is that events today can be live, virtual or a hybrid.

By connecting with people in real-time in a context that they are open to communicating with anyone about, you can initiate strategic connections, build trust, and establish credibility. This just isn't practical on, for example, Facebook.

So, during a business conference there are usually between two and four tracks with two or three sessions per track (in addition to plenary sessions and other social events). You usually choose the track that best fits your area of interest. On the program, for each session, the conference planners provide the hashtag #xyzconf20 for this conference ("XYZ" represents the organization's acronym, "conf" is the abbreviation for "conference," and "20" stands for this being their 20th conference year). Now, let's pretend that you are an attendee at this conference. You show up for the Track 1, Session 1 on Topic A, and you open your laptop, tablet or smartphone to your Twitter application and start following the #xyzconf20 hashtag as the speaker begins. The speaker is fantastic and it's turning out to be a wonderful presentation; you decide to tweet,

```
"Wow! Speaker A in Trk1 Ses1 on
Topic A is amazing! I'm learning so
much! #xyzconf20"
```

Someone over in Track 2, Session 1 on Topic D replies,

> "Oh, really? This session is boring! Speaker D is unprepared and was not what I expected. Where's your session? #xyzconf20"

You see his tweet replying to yours and you reply back saying,

> "We are in the Monarch Room just off the Eastern Ballroom. Seats available. #xyzconf20"

By the end of the introduction by Speaker A, five to 10 new conference attendees sneak into the back of your session, thanks to your conversation with this one individual. This is just one opportunity of the real-time capabilities and benefits of live-tweeting at events, and we have not even discussed how content can be curated, commentated and shared among colleagues.

Hosting Live Twitter Chats

One of the other ways to harness the real-time communication power of Twitter is to become the host of your own chat. All you need is a topic that needs a host on Twitter, or you can ask to become a co-host of another *tweetchat*; a quick search on Twitter will identify if there is a regular chat that occurs on your topic in your region. Then, pick a hashtag and market your Twitter followers, other social networks, email your target audience, and promote the chat through your traditional marketing channels. You can plan to do the chat once for a special topic, or you can do a recurring Twitter chat that happens weekly, monthly or quarterly.

One model for a Twitter chat is to regularly invite a guest expert and plan for an hour for the chat. Like any live event, make sure to remind people about attending the chat, especially on the morning of the chat and right before the chat begins. Prepare six to 10 questions for the guest expert and send them along to her in advance so she has time to think them through for the upcoming chat. At the opening of the chat, introduce yourself, send a link to instructions on how to join the chat, detail the agenda, do a "roll call" (i.e., everyone tweets their elevator pitch in 140 characters or less), greet regular attendees you see who have joined the chat, and provide any special announcements or rules for the chat. Then, introduce your guest expert and begin with your first question (e.g., "Q1: How would you handle business issue X? #urbizchat"). Your guest expert will then reply with their corresponding A1 answer. The best part is that everyone else will begin to retweet your question to their followers, answer your question along with the guest expert, and ask follow-up questions of the guest expert. You should make sure to retweet the guest expert's answers to your followers so that you have a flow of Q&A in your Twitter timeline for archival purposes, and you can feel free to retweet any other chat participants' answers or questions that are particularly cogent. At regular predetermined intervals you then release the subsequent questions. In between questions you can mention some "pull" marketing calls-to-action (e.g., "Follow us on Twitter to get announcements about next week/month/quarter's #urbizchat," "sign up for our enewsletter" or "subscribe to our blog"), or at regular intervals throughout the chat (which can also be scheduled prior to the chat so they automatically go out throughout the hour). Once you have completed your final question (say, Q10) and the guest expert as given their (A10) answer, you can then thank the guest expert for joining #urbizchat, remind everyone to join you next time for the chat giving its date/time (including the guest expert if you know it in advance and the topic), as well as thanking everyone for joining in the chat.

Other great tweetchat tools that I have recently started to use include:

- http://tchat.io;

- http://twubs.com; and,

- http://storify.com (this is a great tool to save transcripts of tweetchats, and has a tool to place slideshows on your own website).

A great example of a regularly occurring live Twitter chat is #smallbizchat hosted by @smallbizlady (Melinda Emerson). It happens every Wednesday at 8:00pm EST/EDT. See her #smallbizchat website for more information: http://w.w3cinc.com/r50PWs.

Chapter 12: Google Plus Your Small Business

> "I Google myself to find out who I am as a person."

> ~Jarod Kintz

What is Google+?

There is a great deal of confusion over what Google+ is; as Google confusingly defines it as a "social network and identity service." From a user's perspective, Google+ is currently (and this may change over the next couple years) a place for deep, rich conversations with her personal and professional connections, controlling not only who sees what with ease but also with whom she communicates her messages (via Circles (i.e., groups of people) or email from directly within the network). And, to a great extent for most business owners, your personal and professional lives can be fluid and distinct from one another. For the Small Business owner, Google+ is a place for her business to build its own brand, obtain great search engine results through good Web presence content marketing and referral networking (because Google+ shows up in Google searches and advertisements all over the Web, unlike Facebook), and drive traffic to the company website for sales. Did I tell you sales happen on your website?

Why Google+?

While you may hear that Google+ is not as large nor active as Facebook right now (remember, Prodigy, AOL, Friendster, Myspace, Yahoo! and every other passé social network?), there are several reasons why you should consider Google+ *now* as part of your primary Web presence strategy over the next few years. By the way, that means that with over one billion registered users (540 million users being monthly active users), Google+'s *active* userbase will surpass Twitter's total *registered* userbase—which took eight or more years to build—of 550 million registered users in 2014, in only *three* years. It will also likely reach Facebook's userbase of monthly active users over the next year or two. The reasons for this dramatic growth and why Google+ now are simple. First, Google "owns" the Web as the most powerful index of websites freely available to everyone with an Internet connection, and it is the global leader in display and search advertising. Next, Google owns YouTube, the world's largest video search engine and social network. YouTube says that it "had more than 1 trillion views or almost 140 views for every person on Earth" in 2011 and the video content on the Web is only going to grow as more businesses and consumers get savvier with new video and mobile video technologies. Finally, marry their success on the Web (Google Search and 500+ other products), the Social Web (YouTube, Blogger and several other innovations in Social Media), and now with their melding of social, mobile and local search capabilities (e.g., Google Wallet, +1 button, Google My Business/Google+ Local, and Google+), Google poises itself to dominate the SoLoMo Web for years to come. This is a when, not if, proposition. Therefore, ignore Google+ at your own peril.

Developing a Google+ Strategy

While a specific strategy for your business cannot be outlined in this general discussion of Google+, there is a broad sets of tactics you can to get started with Google+ that I recommend. To start, learn about all Google products available to Small Business (on your own or by waiting for my upcoming book, *Google Your Small Business* [http://googleyoursmallbusiness.com/]). Google has over 500 products and services and expanding daily; so many that I have made it one of my career passions to provide one-to-one and staff-wide live and Web-based training, Webinars, half-day and full-day public workshops for Small Business on how to use these Google technologies to market and operate a Small Business. Set to be the dominant player in the market for the next decade at least, it makes sense to get your business intimate with Google. Next, educate yourself as a business specifically about implementing the eCommerce tool, Google Wallet (which are the branded products for both eCommerce payments and mCommerce solutions). Third, as I will explain in Chapters 15 and 16, claim your Google My Business/Google+ Local listing on Google Maps, encourage your customers to provide feedback with reviews of your business, monitor and respond to those reviews, and keep the information and offers up-to-date on your Places page. Last but not least, establish your personal Google+ profile and create a Google+ page for your business so that you can start learning about the social network in order to engage your target audience.

Chapter 13: LinkedIn to Your Small Business

"LinkedIn is for the people you know. Facebook is for the people you used to know. Twitter is for people you want to know."

~Unknown

*Create a LinkedIn Profile **and** a LinkedIn Company Page*

Think about your LinkedIn profile as your Web résumé. Complete your profile and update it as necessary as your professional life changes and progresses. Connect with contacts by using the LinkedIn utility to search your e-mail contacts against the LinkedIn network. Forget keeping business cards as your contact management system; use LinkedIn! And, please do not "automagically" send all your Twitter posts to your LinkedIn profile from your company Twitter account without considering the strategic impact of doing so. It makes sense for some businesses (like mine) and not for others!

Your Company page is your business' Web presence on LinkedIn, not your profile. Use this place to highlight your product(s)/service(s) and get recommendations for them, and post updates about positive goings-on as your business grows and prospers. The business can use the status updates for mini-press releases about company's progress and goings-on. This is also where you can empower your employees easily to spread the company's marketing message outward to the LinkedIn community through LinkedIn Groups, and get new hires through their own LinkedIn personal connections. Finally, you can syndicate your Twitter and blog posts to your Company page as well.

- http://www.linkedin.com

- http://w.w3cinc.com/tDZWsx – A great primer on how to use LinkedIn for a job search. Many of the same principles apply for procuring new business contacts!

- Watch the video: "LinkedIn in Plain English" [http://w.w3cinc.com/thTxRT]

I really like the Seth Godin's standard for Social Media relationships when it comes to your LinkedIn personal profile. He says that you should be able to look at your LinkedIn personal connections and on any business trip, send them a message asking them if you could crash on their couch while you were in town overnight. While they may say "no," that's the level of intimacy and trust you should invest in those connections.

Challenges

- Request or write recommendations of colleagues and customers on your Company page for specific products/services. Start becoming active within appropriate industry groups and reviewing LinkedIn Applications that may be useful to you (e.g., "Reading List by Amazon" or "Events").

•   Become a LinkedIn Premium member for only a month or two, so you can see additional information about the people who view your profile, add YouTube videos to every product/service on your Company profile, and syndicate your blog posts to your Company profile.

•   Find me and connect: http://linkedin.com/in/raymond & follow our Company page at http://www.w3cinc.com/linkedin.

Chapter 14: Social Search Optimization

"What we find changes who we become."

~Peter Morville

"If I cease searching, then, woe is me, I am lost. That is how I look at it - keep going, keep going come what may."

~Vincent van Gogh, *The Letters of Vincent van Gogh*

One of the often-overlooked benefits for business in its Social Media practice is the power of Social Search. We think incorrectly that Google is the only Search Engine. And, we forget that every website, social network, blog, and other niche Social Web property has search capability. What this means is, is that you can direct a significant amount of quality search traffic from Social Media to your website (which is where sales happen).

First, Google provides you with three broad Social Search channels: Search, Blog Search and Discussion Search. For Search, here you can optimize your website's Social Media business profiles to be keyword rich and linked to your website to drive Web traffic. I'll discuss this in the next section. Next, if you have a blog by now or you are going to build one from our discussion in Chapter 9, you'll start to see the benefits coming from Google's Blog Search engine. Finally, Google Discussion Search gives your involvement in email discussion forums (such as Google Groups and other Web-based discussion forums) some major oomph by directing traffic from your interactions in those boards and forums. Do not ignore the power of this Web traffic. Recently (as of about January 2014), Google has removed an easy way to view these search results exclusively Blog Search and Discussion Search separate from the standard Google Search, so you have to do a bit of work to see these independent silos' results. You need to go to http://google.com/blogsearch to see the Blog Search, and you use https://www.google.com/?tbm=dsc to do search of the Discussion Search. Now, let's discuss how you optimize your social presence to work Social Media even better.

Most Social Media platforms have the ability to make a business page for your company from your personal login (*a la* Facebook, Google+, LinkedIn, etc.). A question I typically get relates to Twitter, Pinterest and other sites that are not designed like those Social Media platforms. The issue that comes up is with the Terms of Service (or Terms of Use) agreements and whether or not your business is even allowed to be on the platform as a business. My best recommendation is to **read** the agreements before signing up for the service. In the case of Twitter and Pinterest, it was a rough road for them, as they were not designed with businesses in mind, and they had to update their Terms of Service later on after many businesses joined their networks. Most social networks and platforms are aware of this reality now and are writing their terms/agreements with businesses in mind. If you decide you are comfortable with joining that network, you will register a separate account directly with your business email address and use all business information in the process of signing up.

Here's where the magic happens: in the creation of your business social profile (or page) on any of these Social Media platforms, there are several places where you will be able to enter a few key pieces of information. They will have primary fields for your business name, website/blog, a description (typically called a "profile") of your business, and a photo to place a picture of you or a business logo. When you see these fields, you know you need to concentrate on making sure you get all this information correctly inputted and that you have thought strategically about them. Remember our discussions before about the power of keywords and drawing people from their social networking onto your blog (or directly to your website) which is where you control your brand? Well, each of these Social Media platforms has search functionality built into them. We want to make sure these fields are completed with your keyword strategy in mind. Your profile description should have your most important keywords/keyphrases in them. Your picture may even make sense to have a call-to-action in it, as long as it is not disallowed. So, now as a happy user of this Social Media platform, I can search for things I need (your products and/or services) and your profile will appear because you have optimized it for Social Search within your profile.

Protecting Your Handle

During the sign-up process of most Social Media platforms, you will be asked to create a username. This is either your email address, or a separate name you choose. Some people choose their business name or they've used something more that relates to their business. It is a sad but unfortunate reality that there are Web traffic "poachers" out there willing to take usernames (similar to the aforementioned cyber-squatters who register domain names so they can resell them to you at a high price), to capture some of your hard-earned Web traffic. This includes the usernames on major Social Media platforms!

Let's take an example of my personal productivity podcast, *ProdPod, the podcast of productivity lessons in two minutes or less* [http://ProdPod.net]. My username is "productivity" at PodBean.com, which is where my podcast is hosted, and I determined that "productivity" was too lucrative a keyword for my podcast's underlying subdomain at PodBean [http://productivity.podbean.com] than using "ProdPod." I could not believe someone had not already taken "productivity!" It's very possible some unscrupulous individual could have registered the username "prodpod" and could attempt to compete with my podcast's name that way. Thankfully that is not the case and honestly now that I have made PodBean direct visitors from my domain, I'm not all that concerned though I pay attention to my Web analytics to make sure no one is doing that to it.

Your business is much more important than my personal productivity enthusiasts podcast, I can assure you. You do not want to have the legal and financial disadvantages that come along with someone beating you to your business' username. I recommend that you take all those usernames across all the major Social Media platforms. You can use a tool like NameChk [http://namechk.com] that will run your business' username (also called a "handle") across the top Social Media sites and tell you whether it is being used or not. Now, in *most* cases, if someone is using your preferred username you cannot really do anything about it. You choose another username as close as possible to your preferred username and go on with business. However, if you believe that an individual or business is using your copyright, trademark or service mark, or he or she is impersonating you, you should reach out to your business attorney and have him or her look into the matter. Now, with NameChk's list of services for you to register, create a spreadsheet (columns: Site (its name, e.g., Twitter, Facebook, etc.), URL (Web address to the site), Username, Password, Email (address you signed up with), Purpose (what you may use this site for in your marketing strategy), and Notes (for specific descriptions of information you may want to remember about that social site).

This is what I would expect your spreadsheet might look like: http://goo.gl/XlWBE (Google Drive Sheets template). You can actually use this template if you would like; just open it and select the option to "make a copy" into your Google Drive account, or download it in a Microsoft Excel file format to use locally.

You may want to add a column for the login page URLs if it's not easy to find directly from the site. (The grey columns in the template linked above are optional.) Of course, you can customize this layout to your business' needs. This is a base sample I use for my clients and handles 95% of their needs.

As well, you may want to create a separate email address at your business' domain (e.g., social@yourbusinessname.com) so that you do not start to get the *many* email newsletters and impending notifications from these services as you sign up. You can check this email account once a month and just clear it out once you've reviewed it for any actually important announcements. Also, you can check the news media headlines monthly at the same time (or on occasion) for discussions of any new social media services that might establish themselves. You can then secure your profile name for your business and add it to your spreadsheet. Remember, you do **not** need to use all of these services; it's just for social brand protection.

These are services that do this kind of social brand protection for you:

- http://claim.io

- http://knowem.com

And, finally, a word of warning about registering all of these social profiles at once. Google and the other search engines do not like it when you register all these social media profiles all in a concentrated period of time. They think you are trying to cheat their quality control system, even though you are legitimately trying to protect your business's Web presence. I recommend that you plan to register no more than 10 of these social profiles per month; however, if you do not have a website yet, go ahead and secure them all as quickly as you would like before the website launches. With about 150+ major Social Media sites out there right now (and growing), it will take you about 15 months to register them all at 10 sites per month. Namechk gives you the list of sites by priority, so it's pretty easy to know which you need to do first and so on each subsequent month. I think that makes it relatively easy to do in chunks once a month, perhaps even setting it as a repeating calendar event or task. Now, you might be afraid that someone is just waiting to take your business handles, so you believe you need to take them all immediately. You have to take the risk of the penalty by the search engines over getting that business handle; do more research by Googling "black hat penalties" and see whether the penalties are worth your gaining that social profile username.

Part III - Local Search Success

Chapter 15: Local Search Engine Optimization

> "When you don't know what you're searching for, you have to look absolutely everywhere."
>
> ~Holly Black, *The Poison Eaters and Other Stories*

While upon reviewing Part III, you might notice that it has only two chapters. One might infer that that means that Local Search is less important than Social Media or Mobile marketing. And, that person would be wholly incorrect. If I had coined the marketing term *SoLoMo* I would have called it *LoMoSo*. First, it would make the term alphabetical and being myself high on the Type-A behaviors scale that would make me personally happy. Next, I would not have the problem I had several years ago while helping a rabbi understand the concept. You see, I talked for about 30 minutes with the religious scholar randomly at a business event and we seemed to be making progress in his understanding of how it could help his temple. And, then he abruptly stopped me and said, "Why do you keep saying my name? I know my name!"

Shocked, I looked down at the religious man realizing the issue and said, "I am saying SO-LO-MO, not Schlomo!"

The rabbi's first name was Schlomo and he thought I was disrespectfully calling him by his first name the entire discussion. We both had a good laugh after it all, but then I realized that rapidly saying *SoLoMo* was not allowed and enunciating *SoLoMo* was of absolute importance in every presentation I give on the topic. (By the way, I am totally joking about this story!) Finally, and the most important, SoLoMo should really be implemented in the order Local →Mobile →

Social. You build your local Web presence (as I am going to detail here and in Chapter 16), then you establish a mobile communication platform, and finally bring in the people through social listening, speaking and connecting. It's all very interconnected so at some point you won't think about implementing any new strategy without each component in mind, but for ease and for progress' sake, implement one at a time then double back and update your Web presence with SoLoMo components as you learn, have mental and financial capital available, and find time in your schedule.

Local Starts With Your Website

If you're a business that provides products and/or services within any geographic region (town, city, county, state or region), Local Search is important to you. I am going to provide you with a basis for how you should structure your website and where you should get yourself established on the Web in order to capture the best local Web traffic for your business.

But first, while some would argue that "Local Search" sounds like it only matters for hyper-local businesses and not national businesses, I disagree on three points to those entrepreneurs with grand ideas for the growth of their business. First, unless your products/services are provided where people are not connected to the Web or Mobile Web, people are being geographically located by search engines and being given that data back that's most relevant to where they are, not you. The world revolves around your customer not your brand; always remember that. As well, unless Web storage space skyrockets inexplicably in price, it makes sense to capture as much traffic on your website from pockets of local buyers on different segments of your websites. This is far easier than competing with only competitive keywords that may or may not be as relevant to your customer. Finally, if your business does go global and you no longer need a local presence (in your opinion; see my first point), you can always re-develop your website at that point and you will have the resources to re-market your Web presence to the global audience. You must build your home base, then grow.

So, with my response to 99% of objections out of the way (insert devilish smirk here), let us get into the details of what Local Search components a Small Business needs to affect the search engines:

• On-Page Local SEO Basics

• Creating a Targeted Hyper-local Presence

• Local Search Directories

On-Page Local SEO Basics

The area where you have most control over your Web presence is here on your own business website. The aspects that you can work on to make yourself more attractive to the Search Engines are what we call "on-page SEO" tactics. And, since your business is hoping to capture Web traffic in a geographical region, we want to localize the content. Some salient points to keep in mind as you're reviewing and starting your local SEO updates. Many of your buyers will be finding your website as a first stop on their research to purchasing a product, and what they learn on your website will determine whether they buy from you or your competition. Keep this in mind as you are determining your target audience and your sales goals. For example, if you try to force them into an eCommerce (online shopping) environment when all they really want to know is that you carry a particular product or provide a specific service, you will turn away business. Take heed that an estimated one trillion dollars of offline sales per year is influenced by online research; these dollars are spent by people we in the industry call ROBO (research online, buy offline) shoppers. And, as I'll cover in Chapter 21, for more techno-savvy shoppers, do not limit their ability to buy from your website when their need or want can be satisfied from there.

And so, on the topic of building your Local SEO presence, there are a few points about SEO generally that need to be covered. I imagine it was a graphic designer or another creative professional transitioning into the Web world that thought it was clever for readability to use underscores in the file names of images and other media (e.g., your_business_image.jpg). And, over time, it just became some kind of fashionable practice for the unaware. Don't do this! Search Engines are similar to lumbering ogres, as they move slowly and generally crush things they do not see in their path. If you use underscores some of the Search Engines will just wipe your site off their map because they do not see anything after the first word you type because the underscore in Web language is a kind of "Stop!" signal. Use descriptive file names (less than 10 keywords in a row) for every file you have on or upload to your website, but make sure to use dashes (e.g., your-business-image.jpg) instead since Search Engines understand them as separators of words. Also, take note that "titles" of Web pages still matter and you should use those 40-60 characters available to you in titling your pages to be keyword/keyphrase rich.

TIP: If you've seen product information (pricing, stock availability, etc.) and other kinds of specific information appear right in the SERPs, this is what's called a "rich-text snippet." It can be quite powerful in driving Web traffic. Google has their own Web coding for this kind of information, but now Google, Microsoft and Yahoo all use a centralized vocabulary of Web coding for this kind of Web wizardry! Learn more at the links below.

•   This Google Webmaster Tools support articles discusses proper formatting of your product pages for SEO purposes. [http://goo.gl/yMHYP]

•   http://schema.org

And, outside of the other SEO tactics available from a basic Web search (which I won't try to explicate here), a question I get frequently is about on-page SEO keyword/keyphrase specificity. I tell my clients and Small Business audiences that you should always be targeting the Search Engines with each page or blog post (which is essentially a Web page) for **one** keyword/keyphrase. The only exception (and another frequently asked question) is about your home page (typically, yourbusinessname.com/index.html). Your home page is unique in that it should include all your major keywords/keyphrases sprinkled throughout the page's copy with hyperlinks to the pertinent pages they are focused on within your website. Remember, Google and the other Search Engines love seeing internal linkages between content; it connotes importance of the material if it's being hyperlinked from one page to another. And, providing keywords/keyphrases on the home page of your website to internal Web pages has much more flexibility and space than your navigation bar on your website.

Creating a Targeted Hyper-local Presence

Your website with the general SEO components in place can now be focused on your hyper-local (specific geographical region's) targets. First, tailor your website's design to make sure your physical address (if it's something you can publish comfortably) is at or near the top of each page of your website along with your main, **local** phone number. The Search Engines love this information to be able to determine where you are and how you might be a fit for their users searching for products/services. Now, if you cannot or do not want to publish your business address (e.g., if you have a home-based business), then you at least want to still capture Search Engines' attention by putting the cities, regions/counties, and state(s) of your business' main location serves. However, if you can, publish your exact address to be more lucrative to the Search Engines. While the need for a toll-free number is diminishing with every new cellphone that replaces a landline, if you keep a toll-free (8**) number,

you can place this above or below your local
number in small text so the Search Engines
have what they want and your target
audience visiting can use the number they so
choose.

If you have multiple addresses, you just place
your main address on the top of all the pages
on your website with your other locations' city
(or regions, counties, and states) at the bottom
or in the sidebar with links to each page
dedicated to the respective location. These
might even be full sections devoted to each
location if it warrants but make sure your
address is real text (not text in photos,
meaning I should be able to highlight and
copy the text of your address with my cursor)
near the top of the page.

With your Location(s) and Contact Us pages,
you really need to pay attention to everything
you're doing here to capture the attention of
the major Search Engines, with particular
deference (for the majority of businesses) to
Google as they are the dominant Local Search

provider. All the Search Engines give you tools to be able to add mapping functionality to your website. For example, Google gives you the ability to embed maps of and clickable driving directions to your business location. (Google also gives you the functionality to insert **photos and videos** that you can upload directly onto Google Maps of your business, which you should definitely consider if you can show your business storefront, especially if it's not street-facing retail, or would like to show inside your business with your customers using and enjoying your product or service. See http://goo.gl/C4MuL.)

An infrequent but understandable gripe from some Small Business owners is that their location is not properly indexed by Google Maps. There are so many factors that can impede the Google Street Maps Team from properly photographing your storefront. If your office or retail location is in a new subdivision, it may also take Google Maps some time to get you on the map. To get priority (sometimes, just getting yourself in the waiting line), go to Google Maps and click on the "Report a problem" link to explain the issue to Google. Remember, Google's responsibility is not your specific business, it's yours.

If you cannot find your business or streets/roads leading to your business on Google Maps, use the "Report a problem" to let Google know.

Back on your Location(s) or Contact Us pages, you should add your phone number, physical and mailing address, and your contact form or email address on both of these pages. These are the basics of why people come to these two types of pages, so do not forget this primary information for Web visitors and the Search Engines.

Some other local SEO resources to ponder:

- http://www.embedgooglemap.com/

- http://geo-tag.de/generator/en.html

- http://mygeoposition.com

- http://google.com/cse

With your on-page local SEO in good shape, now we are going to supercharge your exposure to the Search Engines. When your customers have a need or want more and more they are asking Google to give them the answer first. And, Google presents them with local results if they conclude the search is for a geographically-based business or a product they can purchase locally. Here are some examples of typical searches that Google will understand typically as local searches:

- orthodontist

- estate planning law firm

- car mechanic shop

Savvier Web users are typing search strings like these local search keyphrases:

- pediatric physician near me

- local printing shop

- copywriting service New York City

With both of these sets of local search keyphrases, Google automatically shows you a map to the side of your search results with local businesses (which I'll discuss in the next section). And, for purposes of on-page local SEO, it shows the organic search results (below the paid ads) that match these keyphrases but slightly different for some of these searches, right? If you think about it, if you typed "orthodontist" into Google's search field and nothing else about a location it still knows you want a local search. So, it shows me local search results here in New York City and you get completely different results where you do your search. Therefore, Google is locating you and adding this data to the search. Where does this location information come from, and how can you increase attractiveness to Google, Yahoo and Bing? Search Engines look for pages that are dedicated to specific keywords or keyphrases. So if they are adding this information to the search string by identifying the user's location from their Web browser, you can increase your odds by helping them know your location. You can add a page for every major avenue/street/highway, neighborhood, town, city, county, state and region that your business services or sells products to on your website. And, using the example that you're a local photographer in New York City, the focus of your keyphrases on those pages may look like this:

- portrait photography New York City

- portrait photographer Houston Street New York City

- headshots Gramercy Park NYC

headshot gramercy park nyc

Web   Images   Maps   Shopping   More ▾   Search tools

About 2,400,000 results (0.93 seconds)

Ad related to **headshot gramercy park nyc** ⓘ

$99 NYC Headshot Special - marvinmansilla.com
www.marvinmansilla.com/
$100 OFF all **headshot** and portrait sessions booked in June!

gramercy park Archives - **NYC** Portrait, **Headshot** & Fash
www.stillmotiondesign.com/blog/tag/**gramercy-park**/ ▾
NYC Portrait, **Headshot** & Fashion Photographer | Blog | Still Motion Desi
Portrait & **Headshot** Photographer | **New York City** | Boston | New Haven

klaus enrique photography: corporate **headshots**: gramero
www.klausenrique.com/**headshots**/10/gallery.html ▾
Klaus Enrique Gerdes is a **New York City** based photographer who speci
headshot photography: actor **headshots**, dancer **headshots**, corporate

Editorial - **NYC** event photographer, **NYC** commercial photo
jaydjackson.com/work/editorial/ ▾
Danny behind the counter in Matt Umanov Guitars. Manager. **nyc** corpora
Friends of Friends at The **Gramercy Park** Hotel. **nyc** corporate **headshot**

New York Headshots   Ⓐ 244 5th Av
www.**new-york-headshots**.com/   New York
4 Google reviews   (347) 843-

Karol DuClos Photography   Ⓑ 400 2nd Av

Source: Google.com

Google shows not only relevant pages but also
businesses' addresses and phone numbers right in SERPs.

Now you will likely have dozens of really
powerful pages with pertinent content about

177

those locations (e.g., perhaps a little history of Gramercy Park and why you choose to locate your photography studio there on the page you focused the keyphrase, "headshots Gramercy Park NYC") for the Search Engines. You do not need to make these pages a part of your website's navigation; they will just sit on your website and snag Web traffic and bring people into your website. If this does not make sense, search Google for "landing pages" and you can find a plethora of articles and examples. The important part is that you localize the content to these kinds of geographical searches that the Search Engines are trying ardently to render correctly for its users. Help them help you.

Local Search Directories

As I said above, maps with local businesses are displayed alongside any results when Search Engines determine your keyword or keyphrase is related to a local search. You want to get your business on the map, literally! Below are the links to the major local search directory listing sites to visit and set up a user account. There you will then be able to complete all the necessary information for your business for the listing they are going to put into their directory. Please complete **all** fields provided, make sure they contain your most important keywords and proofread what you put in there. Remember, this will be the first impression of your business for many new clients.

Specifically with Google, they give you a place to host photos and videos in your business listing. Yes, they give you the opportunity to put your photos and videos (up to five) directly onto Google Maps, where millions of people visit daily looking for products and services...for FREE! This is your opportunity to demonstrate your brand value right upfront to targeted leads for your business. Do not overlook this! As well, Google provides you with some restrictions about who can have a Google My Business listing (though, take note, not who can put photos and videos on Google Maps) so pay attention to the directions on the Google My Business signup page; my own consultancy does not fit the criteria to have a Google My Business page. You now need to expose your physical address as a requirement. So, if you have a home-based business, you must list your address while providing your service areas by city and state, ZIP code or circumferences from a specific location (e.g., five miles from 10001). Unfortunately, too many people were taking advantage of Google My Business. Additionally, a word of warning, because of these ne'er-do-wells, Google has had to crack down further on some businesses abusing the system. So, when Google calls you from their global call centers, *answer the phone*. They may not have an American accent, but that does not mean you shouldn't take heed of their calls. If you do not answer, they will shut your listing down and it could take several days to weeks to make your listing go live again. Last, Google has connected Google My Business to what is now known as Google+ Local, their review service built on top of Google+ after their purchase of Zagat, and you should make sure to pair your Google My Business page. The typical process is to create a Google+ Page for your business and it will identify your Google My Business listing and ask you to connect them.

- Google My Business [http://google.com/business]

- Yahoo! Local [http://listings.local.yahoo.com]

- Bing Local [http://bing.com/businessportal]

- http://getlisted.org

- http://ubl.org

If you would like to see how you appear in local search results, check out: http://adwords.google.com/d.

And, finally, if you are planning on being found by Apple iPhone users through the smartphone's digital assistant, Siri, make sure that you are listed on Localeze (and Yelp, which helps). It is the local search directory that Apple uses to source Siri's local search results.

- https://webapp.localeze.com/extranet/

There are also many established hyper-local directories not to overlook, as they can present you with strong amounts of Web traffic because of their offline marketing efforts on your behalf. See about becoming a member or active with your local convention and visitors bureau, small business development center, chamber of commerce, board of trade, economic development authority, Senior Corps of Retired Executives (SCORE), business improvement districts (BIDs), and/or local professional/trade associations.

Armed with this local SEO strategy you are poised to compete well within your target market. Next up I will show you how to capture Web traffic and stronger leads from review sites.

Challenge

Check out http://www.lightstalking.com/seo-for-photographers-3 and learn more about on-page SEO for your photographs (this is also applicable for videos). While you may not be a photography business, you should still optimize your images and videos, so get versed in SEO for both and reap the SEO rewards!

Chapter 16: Review Sites - Dos and Don'ts

"To avoid criticism say nothing, do nothing, be nothing."

~Aristotle

"People ask you for criticism, but they only want praise."

~W. Somerset Maugham, *Of Human Bondage*

Reviews are an important feedback mechanism that most Small Businesses seem to fear, but of which they could really stand a healthy dose. Feedback is your friend in Small Business. More importantly, it's an amazing source of content that can drive much Web traffic to your business and gird its content engagement without much effort on your part. All you need to do is ask and then pay attention to the reviews. Let us cover how to make the most of Review Sites' power then outline briefly the major Review Sites on which you want to be active.

Getting the Most From Review Sites

Review Sites aggregate your customers' opinions of your products or services. Customers typically do not seek out local businesses' profiles on Review Sites for no apparent reason; they head there because they had a superiorly disappointing experience, received something superbly exceptional in the way of service, product or customer service, or *they have been asked to give a review*. Let us presume that all you can do to control the two former categories is provide improve operations, create more exceptional experiences, and make corrective action for the poor experiences of your customers. Your most important Review Sites marketing strategy is to **ASK** = **A**lways **S**eek feedbac**K**.

Whenever you close a transaction with a client, or your client has the happiest moment during your interactions, you need to be ready to *always seek feedback*. On your invoices, have a standard request that reads, "We at ABC Company always strive to be better for you, our customer, every day. Can you do us a favor and let us know how we're doing by going to XYZ Review Site and letting us know? http://xyzreviewsite.com/mybusinessreviewp age." Do you see how I worded that request? I did not ask for a *Great!* or 5-star review or even for positive feedback. I asked them to honestly let us know how we are serving them as a customer. It has been studied and found that if we ask people to give us positive feedback as Small Business owners, we tend to get less positive than if we just asked for feedback plainly. Also, I have given them a direct Web address to my business' review page. I want to make it as easy as possible for them to reach out to my Review Site of preference to get them to write something.

And The Reviews Pour In...

After you start to receive reviews on the Review Sites we will be discussing below, you now have a few more things you need to do.

1.   Pay attention and read your reviews. You may see a customer you want to write to personally and thank publicly and privately.

2.   Negative reviews need to be addressed in a reasonable time frame and once you have satisfied their real concern, ask them to go back and re-review you. If the feedback is not something that needs to be addressed or can be remedied, this is **valuable** information to go back to your team and make changes in the business to improve so they do not happen in the future. Make these changes prominent in your press releases, email newsletters and Social Media posts whenever you can. Your audience will appreciate that they have been heard, been listened to and made a positive change that will impact your business and their experience the next time they buy.

3.   Search for other reviews on ancillary Review Sites that might be "lifting" (sourcing) those original reviews or new reviews from your current and past customers. Then, see numbers one and two above.

4.   Keep ASK-ing for reviews. The more, the higher your ranking on those Review Sites and presumably the more exposure you will get on Google and the other Search Engines.

Yelp

The granddaddy of Review Sites is Yelp.com and you should certainly claim your business listing on their website. Yelp no longer shows within Google+ Local but it still feeds into Google Local Search (at least at the time I checked before publishing!). Whether you should pay Yelp anything to be "featured" or have additional bells and whistles, I am highly skeptical. You can decide the value of those paid listings for yourself, but I generally do not believe in their value. However, if you are in a highly competitive market, have the budget and see results (increased Web or foot traffic) from paying for a "featured" listing, then I fully support your decision. Yelp is rather good at helping a mobile user (which we will discuss more in-depth in Part IV) find your business when he or she is searching for you on the road or walking down the street. So heed this caution: your business category for your Yelp listing needs to be accurate (e.g., do not be listed as only a "Restaurant" if you are a really a café and bakery). As an avid mobile user, if your category confuses I will just as easily move on to another business if its inaccuracy makes me lose trust in your ability to complete a simple category listing for your business.

Angie's List

If Yelp is the granddaddy of Review Sites, Angie's List is certainly the matriarch of Review Sites. Customers pay to be a member of Angie's List and review service businesses there. You can create a free listing (via https://business.angieslist.com/Registration/Si

mpleRegistration.aspx), or just have a current or past customer who is a member of Angie's List write a review for you and you are added to their directory. Either way, you should claim your business listing and manage it according to the strategy above. Angie's List heavily promotes buying paid add-ons to their service; again, I urge you to choose paying any of these Review Sites unless you believe it absolutely beneficial to your business' bottom line.

Google+ Local

Google+ Local is a melding of Google My Business (from Chapter 15) and Google+ (from Chapter 12) with reviews added for good measure. If you have reviews from your Google My Business listing, Google has added them to Google+ through your Google+ Local listing, and if you have a Google+ Page for your business, you can pair the two (Google+ Page and Google My Business listing) into your Google+ Local listing. Yes, it's confusing, but do not worry. When you set up both, they ask you if you want to pair them and the answer is "yes." If you have already paired them, you do not need to worry about any further action regarding connecting them. And, finally, Google+ Local because of its tight integration with Google+ and Google My Business, you can imagine has strong ties to your strength in Google's search algorithm preferences (even if they deny it!). One additional note is to pay attention to the category of Google+ Page that you create. If you are not a local business category to Google+, you are not going to be able to pair and maintain a Google My Business / Google+ Local listing. Many Small Business clients get flummoxed and aggravated by this reality, but if you do not apply for the benefits of Google My Business / Google+ Local, do not attempt to circumvent the rules. Google is aggressive about shutting down rule-breakers so be forewarned!

TripAdvisor

This Review Site is primarily for the active

business or leisure traveler, so businesses that are focused on or cater to travel and tourism business easily lend toward obtaining reviews from your current and past clients. Speak with your local or regional travel, tourism and convention center bureaus (who may be independent organizations or part of your local or regional government) about special programs, membership and how they can help you garner more reviews and exposure on these travel and tourism sites.

CitySearch

If you live in a MSA (metropolitan statistical area) here in the United States, CitySearch is similar to TripAdvisor for you except they cover much more than just travel- and tourism-specific businesses, and they have a team of their own reviewers who do initial and follow-up reviews of your business, sometimes in the form of articles. You can find out here at http://www.citysearch.com/world if CitySearch covers your area and you can check back on occasion to see as they expand to new MSAs.

Merchant Circle

While a new player in the Review Sites market, Merchant Circle is Small Business-focused and that means it is highly prized in my book to get in and get your business exposed through it. From every small town boutique district to every major metropolitan city center, Merchant Circle has traffic they are garnering from customers who are there to review and Small Businesses that are looking for customers. It also includes a tool to create your own local coupon book, if you can garner new customers through small, first-time buying incentives.

There are so many Review Sites that unless you have someone dedicated to searching for reviews of your business full-time, I suggest that you find good software solutions. Google Alerts [http://google.com/alerts] and TalkWalker [http://talkwalker.com] works well for watching most sites, except Facebook and Twitter. Reputation management software exists that can do the heavy-lifting listening for you so you can manage and respond effectively to only the messages and reviews that are important for your business. Peter Kent, author of *Search Engine Optimization for Dummies*, was so kind as to put together a list of local search directories and mixed in with them are several Review Sites [http://goo.gl/5ucNm]. As well, do not miss checking out these Review Sites:

- http://judysbook.com

- http://insiderpages.com

- http://opentable.com (restaurants)

- http://BBB.org

- http://epinions.com (products)

A Different "Review" Strategy

What I have just been writing about is the idea of generating reviews from current and past customers to create content about your business, brand, product or service on the

Web, which in turn will drive traffic to your website. This is where Sales happens, right? Well, there's another kind of review that works in a similar way but it requires you to do some legwork. It's an underutilized strategy and if you put in the effort, it can be really lucrative. Many websites want to attract you to their site to comment on "things" to create more content to lure the Search Engines. In the case of Review Sites, the thing is your business, brand, product or service. However, websites like Amazon, Barnes & Noble, Epinions, *Consumer Reports,* and *Good Housekeeping* all want you to comment on (i.e., review) products as well to increase their value to the Search Engines. So, here is a different review strategy.

First, you search for the most popular industry-related products (e.g., books, audiobooks and DVDs on Amazon and Barnes & Noble) that you will buy, go to the library or borrow from a colleague. You will read, listen or watch the material and take notes along the way.

Next, you'll set up a business profile on each site on which you plan to write a review. In that profile, you'll make sure that if it allows you to include your business website or blog, you make sure that's included. As a matter of practice, you should complete all the fields in these profiles. And, with that set up, now you can log into that account when you write your review of the material. If I were writing as an attorney on some legal book in my practice field, I would write, "As an estate planning and tax lawyer in my state, I found this book on the basics of estate administration to be...." I would continue to provide a useful review of the materials. As well, I will repeat this process (not copying & pasting the same review, but writing another original review) on each site I have registered that might have that book on their site for review. These sites will now continue to attract new and potential buyers of these materials and they will see my expert opinion, which will lead them to browse on over to my website or blog. Free Web traffic!

Finally, having created some great content I might direct my potential clients to these sites to check out the books and my reviews. They will see the earnest review I wrote and the complexity of handling such matters on their own and if they do decide to hire someone for such services, they will have me *top of mind* when they are ready to do so!

Part IV - Mobile Marketing Success

Chapter 17: Think Mobile First (Strategy)

"Progress lies not in enhancing what is, but in advancing toward what will be."

~Khalil Gibran

Now that I have covered Social Media and Local Search marketing, you have finally made it to the part of the SoLoMo that is actually quite a bit technical but can be extremely rewarding in short bursts, because of the nature of Mobile Media. I will try to be as brief and exacting about the tactics that make up the core strategy for Mobile marketing success. As Khalil Gibran hints above, Mobile is about walking toward the future of your Small Business now.

How do you create a Mobile Marketing Strategy?

Think mobile first is the mantra in every aspect of your current marketing and communications plan. Wait...you don't have one? Well, now is the time to write down a policy of rules and guidelines for you and your staff to know how and when to communicate about your business:

• for crises (develop "holding statements");

• for exciting moments (answer the 5W's & How); and,

• for most conceivable marketing touch-points (remember there is branding/corporate identity, sales, referral networking, advertising, and a media exposure/publicity) components of your business.

As much as possible, try to infuse your marketing plans with impact by taking advantage of the SoLoMo intersection —Social + Local + Mobile. From the prior two parts of this book, you should be adequately positioned to implement these tactics throughout the next few chapters with a strong understanding of this SoLoMo triumvirate. After all, that's what this book is all about, affecting each strata of the Web to get you sales from your business' Web presence.

Next, you must streamline your core brand message from all your marketing collateral into a mobile format that fits your mobile marketing tactics. For example, SMS messages have a limit of 160 characters or less. Twitter should be 100 characters or less. Yes, 100 characters is the *preferred* length, not the 140-character limit, so that Twitter users have enough room to retweet your message twice (or add their own comments with a retweet) without being impeded by the character limitations! In every business, I guide my clients through making sure that they have all the pieces for their business' offline and online brand: brand-enabled business name, tagline, effective domain name(s), elevator pitch for a variety of scenarios, features and benefits statements, capability statement (if appropriate), and a marketing and communications plan. And, you must make sure your plan covers a procedure at all levels of communication to have consistent and responsive messaging with your audiences. Now, you can take each of those components and boil them down to those text-message-sized and "tweetable" phrases. You will use these (or variations of these) phrases often in your Mobile communications.

Next, use all the Web data at your disposal to make better business decisions. If you collect all the data you reasonably can, and put it into a format that makes sense to you, you will understand more about your business than you ever thought possible. From there, you can make good and better decisions from that data in your *think mobile first* strategy.

It's estimated 4.2 billion people on Earth now own a mobile phone. There are currently 7.063 billion people on the planet today. That makes 60% of the global population Mobile-enabled!

Mobile user penetration is nearly 81% in the United States and growing rapidly every day. If you consider the Baltimore-Washington metropolitan statistical area or similar regions, that number reaches a staggering 90% or more.

Digital marketing consultancy *eMarketer* estimates we will have almost 50% smartphone penetration in the US by 2013, and it will reach a phenomenal 74% by 2016. If it's any indication, 95% of you reading this book have a smartphone in your hand or your pocket, and are reading this as an eBook on it! Regions like the DC region with its high-tech corridors, high-income and high-net-worth populations will increase those percentages as well.

So, what defines a smartphone?

- High resolution, usually two-to-four-inch color display (though displays are getting larger)

- touchscreen interface

- advanced, purpose-built operating

system (e.g., Google's Android, Apple's iOS, Microsoft's Windows 8 Mobile, etc.)

• ability to send/receive email

• full-featured Web browser (though limited Flash rendering...Android still does as of version 4.0)

• Access to and the ability to install and run applications ("apps")

• camera that can capture still images and high-definition video

• Global Positioning System (GPS) / geolocation capabilities

• ability to access both Wi-Fi and high-speed mobile broadband networks

Where does the tablet fit?

It currently combines some qualities of the desktop/laptop and the mobile phone. Its verdict is still out but watch the evolving market, along with "personal media consumption" devices such as Amazon's Kindle Fire, Barnes & Noble's Nook, "wearables" (such as smartwatches, tech-embedded clothing, smartglasses like Google Glass [http://google.com/glass/start/], and others. It will likely replace many laptops and personal computers, but the tablet itself won't really change over the next five years, according to Google's Eric Schmidt.

Android Versus Apple

By 2014, Google's operating system, Android, will be on almost 50% of all smartphones, trailed by about 36% being Apple's iOS. There are still other players: BlackBerry, Windows Mobile, and more, but the market fragmentation is becoming more and more of a two-party system. As the world's population increases and certain regions of the globe (including good portions of the United States) go "mobile first," the clear winner will be Google's Android.

In 2010, 6.1 trillion text messages were sent

globally. US mobile users alone sent 2.3 trillion text messages in 2011. This is *even though* the length-restriction on text messages has shrunk (e.g., Verizon has gone to 900 characters, iPhone-to-iPhone users using iMessage is theoretically *unlimited*, and so on). Teens are the biggest texters. If you want to get to parents, text message teens to get their parents to act!

Web marketing still includes a great deal of desktop research that looks like this:

Research →Visit store →Purchase

Your customer will research the product or service they seek, then visit your store or office and purchase at that point.

When you add Mobile Commerce (mCommerce or M-Commerce) into the new marketing paradigm, customers are now doing something like this:

Research →Visit store →Purchase

OR

Visit store →Research →Purchase

The customer has their mobile device on them in these two purchase paths, meaning that they're researching in real-time. While the first seems like the older desktop purchase path, it's uniquely different. Your Mobile Web presence is imperative here to convince your customer, in your store perhaps, that you are the right product or service to purchase. You can no longer exact a pristine 800x600-pixel Web presence with all the controls and presentation quality of your standard website. You have screens as small as one inch by one inch and usually two inches by three inches to convey your core brand message. And, sometimes less than a minute to convey and convince before a customer decides to purchase, or she moves on. This may seem daunting; it is actually a great Small Business opportunity for you to make your core brand messaging more effective by *thinking mobile first*.

Showrooming-Proofing

One of the great downsides (which even I am guilty of in *Big Box* retailers like Target and Barnes & Noble) is that some people will practice *showrooming.* This is a method of researching a product in a store, then buying it elsewhere, whether online, by phone or another brick-and-mortar business), and it is up to you to find creative ways to incentivize shoppers to buy in-store and to make comparison shopping more difficult for them. Help customers sift through choices for the "best value" purchase of your products. The more customizable your products are, the ability to buy your products *in the store* from my smartphone, and the ability to get a product not in stock delivered to my home right from the store, the stronger your ability to compete with and overcome showrooming. Also, do not forget to explain to your customers the importance of shopping local and keeping local dollars in the local economy. Finally, your sales staff needs to be trained to spot someone who is showrooming and positively impact your sales through educating them about the Shop Local movement, your mCommerce website and your shopping parity (e.g., free shipping, custom options online, and 24/7 shopping ability) with other businesses. These advantages will help a *showroomer* stay interested in buying from **your store**.

Remember, *think mobile first* because your customer does.

- http://thinkshopbuylocal.com

- http://www.independentwestand.org

Chapter 18: Getting Start in Mobile

(Hint: You're already doing it!)

"I learned not to confuse 'busy' with 'productive,' but I'm still far too addicted to email to resist its early-morning digital snuggles."

~Chris Hardwick

Small Business owners come to my mobile marketing workshops with wonder in their eyes, usually expecting me to wow them with gadgets and gizmos and doodads aplenty! However, they're shocked frequently to find that I carry my smartphone, laptop (and presenter remote), and my tablet (a Google Nexus 7)—and that's all—to teach them about Mobile Marketing. This is not to say there are not *many* such mobile gadgets in my tech arsenal; I will talk about some of them in the next chapters. However, by and large, your entry into the Mobile world starts in a very familiar place: email. *Email?!* my audiences' faces say, shocked.

"Yes! Email," I reply.

Email is one of the most pervasive marketing tools created by the Digital Age. It's a marketers' paradise and one of the most studied marketing sub-fields today. The primary functions built into almost every smartphone today are: phone and voicemail functionality, SMS/MMS (text, picture and video) messaging, and...email! People do not want to get more email, **but** they certainly want to receive more valuable content.

So, do people complain about receiving too much email? Yes. Do people filter much of their email now for spam and other kinds of junk email? Yes. Do people read valuable content via email? **Yes.** (The standard open rates are between 5-15%, by the way, which is far above direct mail marketing, print and television advertising conversions for far less cost.) Should you contribute to the Internet *chatter* with more spam? No. Most importantly, people read email on their mobile devices. More and more each day, more email is read on smartphones and tablets than in traditional email clients on desktop computers and laptops. In the next few paragraphs I will detail my mobile email marketing model for not contributing to the junk heaps in your past, current and potential customers' inboxes.

Mobile Email Strategy

As I said before, there are many resources for studying the effectiveness of the components of email marketing: how does a subject line increase customers opening your email? Can an overactive email frequency contribute to Unsubscribes? Does the Sender name influence open rates? I will try to provide answers to some of these questions along the way, but my primary goal here is to help you form a mobile email strategy that brings leads and sales to your business through your website (which can include your mobile website, too).

Let's begin with the design of your email messages. I am presuming you know how to send an email message, so I will not get into those basics. So, you need to think about the overall visual message you're communicating with your email before you send the first message. What's going to get me to sign up for an email newsletter of yours? If you skipped ahead, jump back to Chapter 9, to the section entitled, "The Ultimate Small Business Website/Blog Strategy," and read that before moving on here. If you have your website/blog strategy working, people are being added to your email list every week or month in some amount. Check. Next, think about those headlines. This should be quite simple now if you read Chapter 11, "Headlines, Headlines, Headlines." Writing captivating headlines as email subjects and your email list will respond well. Further, you need to visualize how your email will look upon the person opening it. This includes your branding (logo, color scheme of the header and footer and other images), where you place company contact information, tagline, company/product/service descriptions and CAN-SPAM Act information for unsubscribing.

Your content strategy is really where the rubber meets the proverbial road in mobile email. If I open an email newsletter ("e-newsletter") and see one that goes on and on for several paragraphs of dense text, I won't read it now, and likely never will. So, think as long as you would like about the content of your email but write concisely. The email should have three parts to it:

• Beginning: Company news;

• Middle: Valuable insight or resources; and,

• End: Call to action.

In the Beginning, you highlight in a few

sentences what new improvements you are making in your business or exciting products or services have been added this past week or month. Your e-newsletter should be on a monthly or weekly schedule, unless you have a strictly seasonal business where a quarterly cycle is more appropriate. "I don't have anything new happening in my business," you say? Well, you had better figure out something to say that shows your business is viable, growing and showing me *potential*. I do not recommend making anything up, but I recommend that you learn to talk confidently about the happenings of your Small Business. Improvements and action are always happening in a thriving Small Business; it is not a matter of it not existing, it is really a matter of paying attention to and capturing the moments.

The Middle is why I typically, as a consumer, open an email in the first place. This section should be the inspiration for writing the headline that becomes your Subject line of most email newsletters. This needs to be a short and valuable insight into your product or service. How can I best take advantage of your newest product? Is there something in the industry that I should know that will help me or my business gain a market edge? When is the next big date, deadline or event coming up, that I should put in my calendar? Circumstances or your business may lend to speaking tangentially about other topics or industries (e.g., a Virtual Assistant business might give personal productivity, software instructions, or Small Business management advice, tips and tricks).

A great example of this is Paula Tarnapol Whitacre of Full Circle Communications' e-newsletter, *Ease in Writing*. Paula has been active for many years writing this concise and valuable email resource. I am excited each time her email shows up in my inbox. She highlights local businesses with expertise in the areas in which she writes. She gives practical writing tips and techniques for businesses and organizations. As well, she has assembled many of her years of articles into a complimentary eBook that's also available to download from her website [http://fullcircle.org]. I highly recommend you check it out to see that email can marry function and form with the right audience in mind, and create a desire to open an email through valuable content.

At the End, you want to provide your email readers with a Call to Action. Why did you send them this email? What is your end game goal for this person? Now that you have done for them, what can they do for you? For some, that is visiting your website where they can buy your product or service. For others, you want to get them to your Social Media to keep them top of mind when they are ready to buy. And, yet for others, it is to get them to come to your store or business and meet with you. There are many other options and your Calls to Action should vary with your e-newsletter as it grows.

And there you have it, the anatomy of a successful email strategy. I outline this email strategy as a guideline to get you started, and you may find within a few weeks or months that you would like to try different formats. Use "A/B testing" with your lists. And, let the data drive the e-newsletter's evolution for your email strategy. Next up, let us discuss what brings the mobile component to life.

Mobile Email Tools

The not-too-genius reality is that people do not like long email messages to start. So, if you think mobile first when writing your messages you are 80% there with your Mobile Email Strategy. The component that most people miss is your software. As I discussed in Chapter 4, there are several, sufficient email marketing and management software tools. The importance of them is that they help you communicate (i.e., properly adapt) to mobile devices. When I read an email message on my desktop computer or laptop, I have a different way of reading that email (and some statistics suggest a shorter attention span [http://www.emailmonday.com/mobile-email-usage-statistics] since the average attention span is seemingly decreasing [http://www.statisticbrain.com/attention-span-statistics/]) than when I see an email message appear in my mobile inbox. The software you decide on should know when I open your email from a traditional or mobile email client and "automagically" give me the content I want in that perspective. The difference here is that the content you write for me on a traditional email client will be different than what you write for me on a mobile email client. You guessed it. It will be stripped of images (for the most part), it will be more concise writing (boiled down to the essence of your messages), and you will make all the Web addresses and links in the email message "naked." Instead of the saying "click here" you will write it as "click here: http://shorturl.co/nnn999." (See Chapter 3 for our discussion on Short URLs.) You do not necessarily know what mobile email client I am using, so do not take chances that it will be smart enough to read hyperlinks so giving the "naked links" (fully exposed hyperlinks so I can copy-paste them into a browser) is good insurance.

I would like to note that "responsive email design" should be taken into consideration when you decide on an email tool and designing your Mobile Email Strategy. Responsive email design is the principle of coding your email so that it adjusts the height and width of everything in your email to the size of the screen that is viewing it. While the numbers and technology are rapidly changing, I am still holding that an email marketing tool that provides the different format for mobile messages than standard messages is the more effective means for the vast majority of Small Business. I have many issues when opening email marketing messages on my smartphones and if the sender had been diligent with their email marketing, I would have received a clean, plain-text message in my mobile email application (and actually read their email versus what I usually do which is just delete!) rather than a bloated, garbled email message. If you think responsive email design is right for your company, speak to an experienced email marketing consultant before making that move.

The good part about this Mobile Email Strategy is that if you are using an email marketing software tool like those in Chapter 4, you already have the technology in place to make this happen. Now, all you need to do is the mobile formatting and streamlining of your message to make sure your mobile user can read and act on your e-newsletter.

SMS / MMS Marketing

With your local Web presence, Social Media community building and Mobile Email Strategy in place, perhaps you would like to continue down the Mobile Media marketing pathway. Short Messaging Service (SMS) and Multimedia Messaging Service (MMS) are your next avenues. SMS/MMS marketing is similar to an undervalued stock; it's on the cusp of becoming the next big frontier for

Small Business marketing. Once large corporations start making inroads into SMS/MMS marketing, consumers will be deluged and SMS/MMS marketing will become an overvalued stock (which, as you know, is the time to sell). While other companies try and fail, it benefits you to succeed in this powerful marketing medium while it is still highly effective with your target audience. I am encouraged by the development of several SMS/MMS marketing services that have come onto the scene recently trying to bridge the gap for Small Business to have reasonable tools to get their marketing messages out. Unfortunately, I would say that SMS and MMS marketing is still not at a place where a business should attempt this as their **primary** mobile marketing focus without an agency specializing in this media. However, the strategy and tools below will get you acquainted with mobile marketing. Further, I suggest you test the tools to see what they can do before engaging an SMS/MMS marketing firm/agency.

Google Gives You a Voice

Google Voice [http://google.com/voice] is by far one of my favorite products that Google has ever bought, enhanced and provided to consumers for free. (Note: you are not getting rid of your mobile or landline telephone plans with Google Voice. You are merely enhancing your business' telecommunications capabilities for free with Google Voice.) It is not perfect by any means, but it is a powerful tool if you are willing and interested in dipping your toe in the mobile marketing waters. Google Voice is a telecommunications platform, where you can control calls coming to one number that Google assigns you or you can port your existing phone number to Google Voice. When you begin, just take a new *local* number to test it out before porting any existing business phone number to the service (which is a nominal fee). From this "Google Voice Number," you can direct callers based on their Caller ID to any phone you have, whether it is your office phone, home phone, mobile phone or others. The caller never knows from where you are answering (or making) the phone call, so you can control all your telecommunications from that one Google Voice Number. Not only that, you can categorize those callers to get specific voicemail messages based on who they are; your mother and father can get their own messages, your customers another, and your employees yet another message. Additionally, for **free** you can text (SMS) message anyone in the United States as much as you want from your computer/laptop or mobile device through any Web browser. With all the amazing Google Voice abilities, the key features that are the most powerful for Small Business mobile marketing are actually its *SMS* and *click-to-call* functionality.

Let's take a retail business and how I would use Google Voice. First, on my website, I would set up the click-to-call functionality. Google gives you a bit of Web code that you put on your website and now a customer visiting your website can click on the image, put it in *their* phone number and wait for a call from you. In the background, Google Voice calls you wherever you want to be called simultaneously and when you answer it then makes an additional call to your website visitor. It connects the two of you when you are both on the line. This all happens without anyone noticing a difference, but it is phenomenal when you think about what's happening technically. One of the most important marketing axioms we know is that getting your phone to ring is important and **answering** your phone efficiently is even more important. With click-to-call (as opposed to a regular call to your retail business' main number) is that Google Voice attempts to find you wherever you or your staff may be. In turn, the likelihood of your potential customer getting a live person on the phone to buy from you is that much more greatly increased. I have seen several businesses use this feature in very innovative ways to make handling inbound calls a breeze...and profitable.

Next, wherever my customer service representatives are I would set up Google Voice on a laptop (which may already be available if you have a POS system set up on a computer/laptop station), mobile device (e.g., iPod Touch), smartphone or mobile tablet. This means only that you need to log into the Google Voice account in your Web browser. From there, you can use that Google Voice Number in many mobile marketing campaigns and provide feedback by SMS to your potential, current and past customers for sales and customer service. You can have as many people as you need logged into the same Google Voice account for SMS, and the messages do not have to be deleted ever so you have a history of all the SMS communications for reference later. You can annotate ("Add note" in the drop-down options menu) an SMS conversation so that everyone on your team knows what happened or what needs to happen for that client or contact. You can also direct Google

Voice to send those text messages to your mobile phone if you want to receive them directly; when you respond to the messages they show your Google Voice Number, not your native phone number. Note: five identical SMS messages can be sent to recipients at a time (which seems to be about every hour or two) to prevent SMS-spamming. You can get around this, not to SMS-spam, by adding names to the beginning of each SMS text message manually.)

I particularly like that you can email a voicemail message through Google Voice so that your customer service team can forward those messages via email (audio file with text transcript) to the most appropriate team member. He or she can then contact that person directly, or provide back to the customer service agent, with the best response. This can be a huge time-saver for the business and clients if the sales or executive team spends a lot of time not in the office or in meetings. They can quickly check those messages via email and provide responses on-the-go.

Altogether, Google Voice provides (not without limitations here and there) an amazing feature set to create innovative business marketing campaigns not just for call-handling, but also managing SMS campaigns.

Keeping It Brutally Simple

If you *really* feel like you are time-constrained, on a shoestring budget, and not going to get a handle on SMS marketing, take heart that you *can* execute a text-message marketing via traditional email marketing software. All you need is a directory like http://www.emailtextmessages.com. First, ask your customers for their mobile numbers and telecommunications carrier (Verizon, AT&T, T-Mobile, etc.). Then, you can look them up via the above website and add them to your email marketing software's database as the formatted email address associated with their mobile number (e.g., 2125551212@txt.att.net). Now you craft your mobile messages to those email addresses as 160 characters or less. Some text message applications on smartphones receive more characters, but I would keep it to the standard 160-character limit so that everyone sees the same messages consistently. (Remember to review the section on how to write tweets, "Headlines, Headlines, Headlines" in Chapter 11; simply write your messages excluding the hashtags.) Don't forget to give your customers an unsubscribe option! It can be as simple as saying, "Text STOP to unsubscribe." If the texts are valuable enough, hopefully, you will not receive many of those in your marketing campaigns.

- Mobile Marketing Association's *Consumer Best-Practices Guidelines* [http://www.mmaglobal.com/node/1640](review Section 3 on Advertising Programs, pages 42-45.)

Moving Forward With SMS

From advertisements and cereal boxes to reality TV shows, you have likely seen requests to text message to a short mobile phone number (called a "short code"). You can vote now for your favorite talent, request more information about a brand/product, send client appointment reminders, alert your best customers to special discounts, or donate money to your desired charity, all via text message thanks to these short codes. Short codes can come in many styles and sizes; you can have vanity short codes (such as COKE, ABCTV, CHASE, 2HELP (American Red Cross), CNNTV, ARBYS, ASPCA, GOOGL (Google), and many more) or you can have random short codes. You type these short codes (as their corresponding numbers on the *numeric* keypad such as 2653 for COKE, 22288 for ABCTV, and so forth) into the "To" (recipient) field of your text messaging application on your cellular phone. These vanity or random short codes are considered "dedicated" short codes to one entity/organization, while you can also have "shared" short codes. These shared short codes can be leased *only with* the use of a "keyword(s)" (with which you can also lease vanity keywords). So, why all this technical information about short codes? These short codes are at the heart of a very powerful SMS marketing tool for Small Business which I am going to outline the strategy for below.

- http://www.usshortcodeswhois.com/

SMS Short Code Marketing Strategy

If you believe that you are ready to launch an SMS marketing campaign, I would recommend that you start with short codes. I am going to outline the strategy without focusing of any specific service; however, you should be able to implement this strategy using any of the other competent services available listed below. Also to note is that while EZTexting [http://eztexting.com]is not the prettiest interface, it is my favored service for being reasonably-priced and it gives you all the necessary functions without having to work with a telecommunications carrier to lease very expensive short code registrations for dedicated or vanity short codes. Finally, start with random codes and pay for the keywords when your business is ready to run its first full-fledged SMS campaign. While some or all of this may not make much sense right now, come back to this section once you begin implementation of your SMS marketing strategy. You will be glad that you did.

As promised, here are a few SMS Marketing tools to research and see what you are looking to achieve:

- EZTexting.com

- Fanminder.com

- TextAlert.com

- MobileCommons.com

- MobiQpons.com

No matter what tool you use, remember to use the tool yourself for as long as it takes for you to get comfortable with how it works. Building your mobile opt-in list through short codes campaigns gives you a powerful open and conversion rate opportunity for your business. This is not something to be left solely to an intern, or delegated completely to a staff member, without you having at least a basic user knowledge and experience with the tool in which you are going to invest.

In developing your SMS marketing strategy, you will want to answer the following questions:

• What do you want your customers to do? (Call to action; long-term not just with one text message response)

• What are you giving them, of value, to join your mobile opt-in list?

• What are they giving you, of value, in return for your value?

• How will you define success of your SMS Marketing Strategy? (e.g., new business, greater brand loyalty, etc.)

These critical questions will help you define your core strategy to build your mobile opt-in list, and will help you execute your SMS Marketing Strategy, tactic by tactic. SMS is about the private, personal conversation with your customer: one by one, one to one. How are you communicating with your customers in this intimate way through these tools?

And, finally, take heed that SMS is an undervalued stock and it's *buy, buy, buy* time now. But, do not put all your eggs in this one basket as its time will come and you'll need to be ready to move on this data for marketing longevity.

Mobile Advertising

One tried-and-true way of Mobile Marketing is to advertise through mobile ad networks. If you jump back to Chapter 7 you will find our discussion on Web advertising and I will not give this section much focus. There are a few modifications to any Web advertising campaign that is concentrated more on mobile devices than for regular Web browsers. First and foremost, *think mobile first* when it comes to functionality, message and customer experience. There are functionalities in mobile messaging you should research, such as "click-to-call" [https://www.google.com/ads/innovations/ctc.html] that Google developed but other platforms like Yelp has and Twitter began testing recently. When it comes to customer experience, do not lead your customer away from your mobile website unless absolutely necessary. Mobile ad networks can be as easy as checking a few different selections on the Google AdWords platform and designing a mobile advertisement, or it can be as complex as choosing an entirely mobile-centric advertising platform (as the ones I note below with more unique advertising models).

Platform

There are several competitors to Google AdWords as a mobile advertising platform, but they still remain the dominant player in the mobile ad publishing market. Their pricing and bidding structures range and I will not get into that in this book as each mobile ad network should have their pricing and bidding in detail on their website, or you should be able to call and get it explained to you by phone. Choosing your platform will require touching base with the mobile ad networks that are out there and asking them for data showing that your audience is there and how they have seen your industry profit from their advertising with them. Some of these mobile ad networks are Google Mobile Ads [http://www.thinkwithgoogle.com/products/mobile-ads.html], Adagogo [https://www.adagogo.com/], mFlyer [http://moasisglobal.com/solutions/mflyer/], AdLeads [http://adleads.com/], and DropIn [http://dropin.io]. Also, note that in many ways Facebook Ads, LinkedIn Ads and Twitter Advertising are all forms of mobile advertising as well, if much of your target audience is accessing these platforms via mobile (which they likely are).

Additional Reading

•   "What kind of campaign will YOU run?"

[http://www.usshortcodes.com/about-sms-short-codes/sms-marketing-examples.php]

- *SMS Marketing for Small Business*
[http://www.eztexting.com/mailers/SMS-Marketing-For-Small-Businesses.pdf]

Chapter 19: Facebook for Mobile Marketing

> "Social networks do best when they tap into one of the seven deadly sins. Facebook is ego. Zynga is sloth. LinkedIn is greed."

> ~Reid Hoffman

Most of Facebook's users use the Facebook mobile app. That is, they download the app to their smartphone and connect to Facebook not through a Web browser but directly within Facebook's own user-experience-branded environment. Also, if you're not holding one of the 2,500+ smartphone models on the market today capable of using the Facebook mobile app, you can always browse to http://m.facebook.com to experience the mobile Facebook environment from your phone's Web browser. Pretty powerful stuff!

And, people are spending more and more of their time in the mobile app than they are logging into their desktop to view Facebook.com. It's quite logical, really. As the more technological capabilities come to your smartphone, the more likely you'll want to connect with your friends and family while you're on-the-go.

Take, for example, your average twenty-something's Friday night: they get done with work and they plan to hit the gym. That ill-fated goal does not come to fruition because a colleague down in the marketing department asks our twenty-something to come out with a group from work to happy hour. Well, they're all going to open up their Facebook mobile app on their smartphone and post an update that they're doing so, inviting any friends to join them. A friend from college chimes in and says they're going to be in town and maybe she or he will join. Great! Off our twenty-something goes and more posts are to ensue throughout the night; perhaps a photo of the impromptu college mates' reunion and some coworker photos are snapped and posted to share among those in attendance. Friends and family may celebrate the end of the week vicariously through the happy hour happening for the twenty-something. You see, the use of mobile social networking extends the power of connecting digitally (and feeding Millennials' ego-driven lifestyles), but it also has the power to create offline relationship-building equity.

For business, Facebook (or any social network that has gone mobile with an app) has the ability for you to engage your target audience through the mobile app. You should review your Facebook Page to make sure that the visual branding you've set in place (cover photo, profile photo and other elements) all look good on the mobile screen. I recommend that you ask your friends and family who have different models of Apple iOS, Google Android, BlackBerry, and Windows smartphones, to look at it and give you their perspective. Most often, Facebook Page coverphotos' text looks too small on a mobile so make it large enough to read on both large and small screens.

On the flip side, Facebook has empowered business by creating a standalone app for you to download that is called Facebook Pages. It is just for you to manage your business' Facebook Page(s). So, if you're not a Facebooker in your personal life, you can download this Facebook Pages app and manage your Web presence there without the distractions. As a side note, if you engage your Social Media community solely on Facebook, look into the Events functionality on your Facebook Page. However, if you're not highly active on Facebook, using the Event app is not fantastic enough to manage your event marketing from there. I recommend that you go with public tools such as Google+ Events [http://plus.google.com/events], Eventful [http:/eventful.com/], or Eventbrite [http://eventbrite.com/].

One point about the Facebook Newsfeed

algorithm is that it seems to have an initial standard of about 10 "Likes" on a post to keep it from being shuffled away as unimportant to your fans' Newfeeds. You should make sure to have 10 people (inclusive of yourself) ready to "Like" your posts to give it a winning chance of being seen by more of your audience. And a final point about the Facebook Newsfeed is that is biased against the Facebook Page. Said another way, it will show more posts from friends than from your business. Facebook is interested in making money from user engagement, not making you money necessarily from user engagement. So, Promoted Posts are now a part of your marketing budgeting if you plan to really be effective (and do not already have a strong community built) on Facebook.

Facebook Checkins (FourSquare Competitor Alert)

Quite simply, as I state further in Chapter 20 about FourSquare and its ability to drive people into your store, the same applies here for Facebook Checkins. You need to determine where more of your audience spends their time, Facebook or FourSquare, and that will make your decision easy about which tool to use...first. Read on to Chapter 20 and I'll explain how FourSquare checkins work and then you can literally swap out Facebook for FourSquare to understand its practical application here. And while you may hear from naysayers that Facebook Checkins is a fading feature, just remember that because of Facebook's size everything on Facebook is not to be ignored from a tactical perspective.

Optimizing Your Website (and Posts) for Mobile

On standard websites, I have what I've called the "Three Click Rule." Your Web visitors want to be able to do or access whatever they visited your website (no matter where they entered your website!) via three clicks. If they cannot in three clicks, they will leave and visit likely your competitors' website! With that, re-structure the links on your website to make this possible for at least all major functions and information accessibility, or suffer the loss of business until you realize the Three Click Rule is vitally important. Now, we are discussing Mobile, and that whittles us down to what I call the "Two Click Rule." You guessed it. The Three Click Rule is shortened—like most things—on mobile websites. Your target customers (on those phones' small screens) want to be able to access or do what they want in even less clicks. Make sure that your mobile website, whether you are planning to build one soon or you have one in existence connected to your standard website, is set up for the mobile user in mind.

As we discussed earlier about website traffic, we are active on Facebook to engage our target audience to *leave* Facebook (in this case, their Facebook smartphone app) and come to our website (which is where sales happen, right?). However, if you post links knowing that many people are reading them on their mobile phones and they're being taking to standard websites not optimized for mobile, you're asking for a problem. This is where having a website that dynamically sends you to the standard or mobile website because it knows what kind of Web browser is loading, can be really helpful. However, if you have independent sites for content, just take that into consideration.

Chapter 20: Getting Your Mobile Website Launched, Apps and Social Location Services (like FourSquare)

"The Mac defined 'personal technology', and the iPhone defines 'intimate technology' as a convergence of communications, content and location."

~John Sculley

"Location is the key to most businesses, and the entrepreneurs typically build their reputation at a particular spot."

~Phyllis Schlafly

You understand now the value of having a

mobile website from the prior two parts of this book. However, if you are not yet convinced or just plain do not yet understand, I will review the highlights of a Mobile Web presence before moving on to the how's. The Mobile Web is a new strata on the World Wide Web; with its own data and own means for being found (ergo, on mobile devices specifically). More importantly, it is a vastly untapped landscape for Small Business staking their claim to mobile website real estate. Honestly, I do not know why there has not been a "Gold Rush" on the space yet by many more tech-savvy businesses, but that is a discussion for another book. Google and the other Search Engines have decided to stratify searches done on mobile away from your typical blended searches (basic text, images, videos, blogs, and more) that you see when you see a search engine results page.

I will pause for a moment to take note that some Web developers and designers make it a point to say that the "m dot" sites (i.e., separate mobile websites from the main websites) are passé or unnecessary with responsive design available (i.e., the ability for the same website to detect and adjust to fit the Web or mobile browser that's loading it). However, I would look at all options before you make a decision. As I detailed in the prior chapter, deciding on what content your audience sees (especially a time-constrained and fickle one) is important and so your decision to always show **all** the content from your main site to a mobile audience may be overwhelming and bounce more traffic than it keeps. Please keep this in mind.

So, with this new mobile reality you can easily be the most visible business to potential buyers if you stage your business' Mobile Web presence effectively. This leads me to my final point about mobile websites: someday soon—very soon—your mobile website will be the first way most of your customers will be introduced to your Small Business. Instead of a business card, potential customers and everyone they are connected to potentially will experience their initial brand exposure via your mobile website. This critical first impression is not to be overlooked by Small Business to succeed in the 21st century.

Getting Mobile-ized

After you make the decision to launch your mobile website, or mobile-enabled website, here is a workflow to follow to make sure you cover all your bases:

1.   Know your business' marketing material well and shrink it to its absolute core, as we discussed in Chapter 18.

2.   Give some thought to your consumer's mobile behavior, brand loyalty, reading habits, learning styles, and check out your competitors' mobile Web presence. Use this actionable information in establishing your mobile website.

3.   Get a good project management tool in place. Asana [http://asana.com/], Trello [http://trello.com/], Mind42 [http://mind42.com] or another Web-based tool to chronologically or visually lay out the

process:

A)   Gather data/content.

B)   Assess your current mobile exposure to the Search Engines.

C)   What are the current, available Mobile Web solutions?

D)   Figure out how you (or who) will design the mobile website.

E)   Determine how many rounds of review of design and content you will have for your new mobile website.

F)   Test, test and test again your mobile website on a variety of devices and scenarios to get a good idea of how your customer will experience it; it may not be great if you live in a rural or suburban area of America that does not have good cellular service, but it will get better over time.

G)   Set a date to deploy the mobile website and make sure to set up good publicity around it so that local news media and the local and industry blogospheres know it is launching.

H)   Finally, create a feedback mechanism for all parties, to include your staff, your developers/designers, your customers and vendors.

4.   Pay close attention to cross-browser functionality and accessibility of your mobile website. (See http://www.w3.org/WAI/mobile/) The more of both, the greater your appeal will be to the Search Engines.

5.   Pay very close attention to your graphic elements. Visuals and typefaces on mobile website are even more important on mobile websites because those are typically scarce and so stand out. And typefaces (fonts) either help or hurt legibility on mobile screens. Choose both wisely.

Because of the wide variety of ways that you can launch a mobile website, please note the broad instructions for launching a mobile website. You can learn about options at this Google-sponsored website, http://www.howtogomo.com, and see how your current website is set up.

Getting Your First Apps Published

There will come a day when smartphones will be pervasive, even in the most rural areas of the United States and the world. I see the groundswell of new technologies touching every aspect of human life as I travel around the United States talking to audiences. And, when that happens, I want to make sure your business has an "app." These mini-portals into your business are going to be the way in which your customers interact with your brand, primarily and personally, and potential buyers possibly find your business (from the various app stores built for each smartphone OS). In a way, they will replace how our websites have been the way in which our customers find new businesses when a need or want arises. The success or failure of your app will be how practical and accessible your app will be for your target audience. (This is no different than your website, right?) It may seem like a daunting task to design, develop, publish and maintain a smartphone application, but the technology market is exploding right now with services to make it a relatively simple project to get something into the app stores. Here are several resources to get your business an app that can be easily and centrally managed by you and your team.

- http://www.appizon.com/

- http://www.biznessapps.com/

- http://www.zdnet.com/blog/small-business-matters/14-diy-mobile-app-development-resources-for-small-businesses/2288

- http://mobiforge.com

- http://wurfl.sourceforge.net

- http://google.com/gwt/n

- http://validator.w3.org/mobile

- http://iphone4simulator.com

- http://iphone5simulator.com

- http://developer.android.com

- http://developer.apple.com/devcenter/ios

- http://developer.blackberry.com

- http://msdn.microsoft.com/en-us/library/ff402535(v=vs.92).aspx

- http://bsquare.com

- http://utest.com

- http://mixpanel.com

- http://google.com/analytics/features/mobile.html

Social Location Services: FourSquare, SCVNGR, and more.

Just as some businesses embraced *Facebook as a Website*, if they found their entire audience was there already, some Small Businesses (with or without knowing it) are taking a *SoLoMo as a Mobile Website* approach by adopting Social Location Services. At first, I took a pretty harsh approach to this *Facebook as a Website* model of establishing a Web presence; instead of doing the work of setting up a website, businesses just created a Facebook Page and used that as their sole Web presence. To which all I could say at the time was "Good luck with that!" Now, I warn against it, but I recommend that those businesses track sales and have a backup plan when (not if) Facebook becomes passé and a new social network (read, likely to be Google+) takes over as the most popular social platform *du jour*. As it relates to *Social Location Services*—the mobile websites and apps that allow you to use the geolocation services built into smartphones so that you can share your location with friends and family and others where you are, and other information along with it—I think there is a valid case use for Small Business to use them as a pseudo-mobile website instead of developing your own. The logic is that you already have (or should have) a website so you are controlling your most important sales tool, but you are outsourcing the mobile component to a place where mobile users are already adopting the technology. The key to your Social Location Services strategy is to make sure that you are effectively incentivizing your community to interact with your location on the platform that leads them to your website, or to engage with you or your staff in real time and space, to keep you top-of-mind when they are ready to buy your product or service. *What would entice you to come to your business location every day as your customer, and do something?*

Chapter 21: Connecting Your Offline Marketing to Your Digital Marketing

"With a healthy movement between online and off, your business can find people where they are, not just where you're most comfortable."

~Chris Brogan

From this point forward, this book becomes quite *future forward* sounding so if you feel like you have enough on your plate with just the first three parts of *SoLoMo Success*, I would stop here and jump over to the Epilogue, then come back to here and Part IV in about nine months to a year once you have had time to implement much of what you plan to do from reading Parts I through III. However, if you feel like you can handle it, persevere on here through Part IV. It is a fantastical and amazing world of social-local-mobile technology and I am eager to share this with Small Business owners willing to take advantage of its power and earnings potential for greater *SoLoMo Success!*

In this chapter, I will discuss QR code strategies for connecting your offline marketing to your digital marketing efforts.

QR Codes Are Almost Dead

So...I will not call QR codes totally dead, but they're on life support for Small Business marketing. I am a huge proponent of them for so many reasons (which is why I am — notwithstanding their seeming demise — still including them here in this book), but the will of the consumer reigns. They have lagged in usage and lacked in popularity to the point of investing in them as of this writing is not necessarily recommended. However, in case you have a situation where you believe these will work or have an undying desire to help prove me wrong, I have chosen to include an explanation of strategy and some basic instructions.

What Is a QR Code?

The basics of a QR (Quick Response) code are that they are 2D bar codes that can turn combined letter, number and symbol characters (such as a hyperlink) into a scannable image, as shown above. The regular UPC bar codes you see at the grocery and other retail stores are 1D bar codes. And, 1D bar codes contain a limited set of information while 2D bar codes allow you to add more functionality to the scan than just the 1D bar codes can. Here is an archived Webinar that I gave on QR codes that should explain most of

what you need to know about them: "QR
Codes for Small Business"
[https://vimeo.com/64653611].

Personal Use of the QR Code

I will give you some examples of how a
consumer might use the QR code outside of a
marketing ploy by a Small Business. I think
this makes more sense, just so you can see
how versatile the tool really is. As a consumer,
I will eventually QR code-label all of my home
digital and other equipment (think, my DVD,
DVR, laptops, microwave, refrigerator, and
smart TV) so I can easily access their online
manuals with a flash of my smartphone
camera using a QR code scanner. So, when my
universal remote will not work the way I
thought it did, I can just scan the QR code on
it and quickly retrieve the instructions on its
proper usage. When my refrigerator's water
filter malfunctions, again, I just scan the QR
code and I can be taken to the manufacturer's
maintenance, repair and parts website. I
might even add an additional QR code that

links to the warranty that I scanned and put into my cloud storage folder.

Think about this: every physical book you own likely has a bar code on it. Go ahead, download a QR code scanner like RedLaser [http://redlaser.com] (which has versions for both iOS and Android) onto your smartphone now and then scan a book's 1D bar code. If you use the Amazon mobile app, you can scan and find almost any product with a UPC label in the Amazon store, and of course, purchase it.

If you use a service like Goodreads [http://goodreads.com] you can scan and upload your entire library to the service for tracking and sharing with others. In this way, you can have a full inventory for your home insurance in case of catastrophe, as well as managing a lending library if you have a large book collection.

The options are endless to bridge the digital-physical divide with QR codes.

In a business setting, all of the above may apply as well, but I will focus on the inventory side of things as the sample use. Say you are a small retail shop on Main Street, and you have inventory from many different suppliers. You may want to add QR codes on your master inventory checklist so that your staff or you (if you are a "solopreneur") can easily jump to a vendor's website product page when you are reviewing low inventory reports.

As well, you can place a QR code on every piece of equipment that you and your staff share or has consumables in the office. Every month you buy toner for the printers. With the snap of a QR code, you can assign that QR code to launch the mobile product page of your preferred vendor's website. Enter in your quantity, payment details and purchase. The productivity opportunities are not just priceless, they are very easily calculated into true Small Business time savings!

Finally, and speaking of money, take your QR

code to the bank, or rather, take your bank with you! When I managed many different bank accounts for a prior business, I would have loved to have had smartphones and QR code apps! What you can do is place small QR codes on the backside of your bank/credit cards. The QR code can direct you either to the mobile website of your bank or to your bank's mobile app on your smartphone if they have one (and most do today). Now, if you are away from the office and your card has an issue, you can quickly scan the appropriate bank card and be taken directly to the site or app that can help you. Additionally, I would create a master QR code sheet (or card that will fit in your wallet/purse) with all the bank and credit accounts. If you find that your card has been lost or stolen, you can quickly refer to the list and scan that QR code to launch a phone call to the Lost/Stolen contact associated with that bank or financial institution. In those critical moments, who wants to search for those numbers! Again, here, QR codes can really be handy for the

Small Business owner.

QR Code Marketing Strategy Explained

So, with all these handy operational ways QR codes can help you in your personal and business life, how can it help you in your SoLoMo marketing? Let us walk through the important criteria for QR codes in the context of SoLoMo marketing and a very basic overview of how to implement a strategy.

What QR Codes Are for in Small Business Marketing, and What They Are Not for

QR codes, in the context of Small Business marketing, are for tracking location and the impact of that traffic that aggregated from that location's marketing message. Otherwise, the QR code's data that you gather will be watered down and you might as well simply put a short URL next to your marketing message. (TIP: Always put a unique, short URL below the QR code, just in case your audience does not want to scan (or the QR code scan does not work for them) but does want to access your marketing message.) Remember that for the consumer, before engaging with your marketing message and getting the value out of the QR code, they need to be educated quickly about what a QR code is, install software if they do not have it on their smartphone or mobile device, and then they can execute the scan. Whew! It's a jump through hoops, but if you make it worth their while, they will do it.

Below I have defined several scenarios where QR codes can work well. But, back on why not to put QR codes on moving or things people generally toss. If you truly want to gain benefit from QR codes on flyers, you would need to put separate QR codes on each individual flyer and be able to track when you handed them out and to whom. Do you have time for that? I didn't think so. Most QR code generators (of which I have listed several at the end of this chapter so you can test them out) give you the ability to access Web traffic from QR scans; these reporting tools usually including how many scans ("hits"), at what time, general location data and so forth. QR codes are much more helpful if they are in easy to spot and use locations where people might be thinking about buying your product or services. QR codes inside the lid of my garbage can to buy more liners when I take the used one out and realize I need to purchase more. The physical proximity of the QR code to the product makes sense, but a QR code on a flyer handed to me in the store about garbage can liners does not. I will likely throw that flyer away as soon as I get to the nearest recycling bin. Further, if I keep the flyer, I am usually taking it to my home or office, at which I have access to computer or laptop with a full-sized keyboard and the practicality (and all the effort you put into creating/designing the QR code) are useless to person holding the flyer. I will just type in the URL provided to access your marketing message. Two final notes about QR codes before we go into the practical QR code methods: they are not for the back of your business card, on your website's home page, on your brochure, or other similarly conspicuous moving and virtual marketing collateral; and tracking your QR code data is really important. If all they do are leading people to your website (especially your main website and not your mobile website; it might be worthwhile if they take them to a download screen for your mobile app), so don't waste their time with a QR code. You can just show the URL. QR codes (without some thoughtful design and testing) are not very attractive to me; those black-and-white 2D bar codes should not compete with your company's logo and other marketing images. As well, you should create a spreadsheet workbook (in Microsoft Excel [http://office.microsoft.com/en-us/excel/] or Google Sheets [http://docs.google.com]) and at minimum track each QR code hyperlink you use to generate the QR code, where the QR code is physically located, where it terminates, and some of the basic Web traffic reporting statistics (which you would check and add to on a regular basis). It is important to know that two people scanned the QR code in week one, 32 people scanned it in week two, and 86 people scanned it in week three, so that you can see trends and take advantage of this Web traffic.

QR Codes at the Register

The first place I recommend affixing a QR code is right on your retail store counter next to each and every register. The QR code would direct your customers to "Like" your business Facebook page, or follow your business on Twitter, or leave a review on Google+ Local, or Yelp. If they did so, right there in front of you or one of your store clerks, then you would give them 5-10% off their purchase that day. You can teach the customer all about what a QR code is, and help them install the requisite software should they need assistance. And, they are given incentives to do it there right then because they will get an immediate reward for it. There is also the added benefit of anyone else within earshot in the store watching the positive commotion will also realize and probably install the QR code app before coming to the register to get their savings discount. Word travels fast when money can be saved!

QR Codes on the Front Door

There is nothing more frustrating than rushing to your favorite local gift shop after work before a major holiday to purchase a gift only to find that it is closed. One way to ease my potential shopper's frustration is to put a QR code on my "We're Closed" sign that leads them to our online shop with a discount code underneath the QR code for free shipping for orders over X dollars. You would include marketing language to explain the deal and visual instructions on how to install and scan the QR code beneath your offer. Now you are making money even when the store is closed!

QR Codes on Signage

If your municipality allows such signage on the street (or if you have advertising on a billboard), you can place QR codes on these items for passersby to scan. Here you want to engage the consumer to scan your QR code to get more information about how to interact with your product, find your store (and if they do, they can also scan that QR code on your retail store counter and score a discount on today's purchase!), or have more information sent to them about your product/service. Since the passerby has the least incentive to do anything with your QR code in this scenario, the value has to be much higher than otherwise.

Should I Use QR Codes on my Products?

There are always exceptions to rules, such as my mine about QR codes for marketing being only for stationary use. If you sell printers and you want to place a QR code to your mobile website that launches their exact ink or toner refills page, I would say "yes," that is an appropriate use of a QR code on a product. This does not really break my rule, though, because printers do not get up and walk around that much; it is pretty stationary. The problem is that you would need to have each printer have its own individual QR code so you can track those specific customers and printers together. So, should you be able to do that in your manufacturing and fulfillment process, go for it. That could be very valuable data.

If your client has purchased a greeting card from your shop and you put a unique QR code on the back of every card, you can track scans that lead to website views but you learn no more practical information about the purchaser than if they just visited your website. Also, if you did want to track every version of greeting card that lead to another greeting card sale, the data you would need to collect would be of Hallmark Company volume for it to be really useful. Stick with just putting the website to your company on the product and let them browse to it and shop the greeting card selections. The effort of putting individual QR codes on each and every product outweighs any payoff in data and any convenience you afford your customer (who likely will not use the QR code from the variety of businesses I have spoken to who have tried over the years).

Additional Reading

• http://bitly.com (URL Shortener, QR code generator and analytics)

• http://goo.gl (URL Shortener, QR code generator and analytics)

• http://www.scanlife.com/case-studies (Largest QR Code supplier to major corporations; it's worth checking out the case studies on their website)

Part V - The Future of SoLoMo for Small Business

Chapter 22: Image Recognition Technology

"The future is there...looking back at us. Trying to make sense of the fiction we will have become."

~William Gibson, *Pattern Recognition*

Arguably, Web 3.0 (or what is known as the "Semantic Web") is the future, but it does not seem to be gaining as much media attention as the technologies I am going to discuss in this and the next few chapters. But, it is good for you to understand what it is and that is coming...eventually. The Semantic Web encompasses a new stratus to the World Wide Web because it is a space where computers collaborate with humans to create information. The Social Web allowed us to connect with one another in a new, interactive way on the

World Wide Web; the Mobile Web does the same just via always-on, always-with-us mobile devices. There are new Web 3.0 standards being developed every year, and their goal is to guide the addition of that final component where humans communicate with computers connected via the Web in a seamless manner and computers are contributing to data production as we need them to. These technologies I will be talking about are the beginnings of the Semantic Web and are the technologies to watch that have the most Small Business marketing potential.

Image Recognition

Image recognition is one of these technologies that has the potential to revolutionize your Small Business. This is the ability for a camera embedded in a device (such as the one (or two) built into your smartphone) or attached to a computer (similar to the webcam attached to your computer/laptop) to recognize a physical object and identify it. Practically speaking, that physical object could be a product, movement or you. Amazon and eBay both have been using this kind of software for some time now in their smartphone apps. I use it regularly to showroom when I am at bookstores and Big Box retailers. I open the Amazon app and snap a photo of the book cover, which renders the Amazon product page for that recognized book. Within two to three clicks, I can make the purchase. Powerful stuff, right? Google and Facebook have this technology in its social networks' photo-sharing tools. It allows you to tag people you know in pictures. A relatively new iOS app called Pounce [http://www.pounce.mobi/] partners with retailers (mostly big retailers right now) to allow customers to photograph-and-detect products in print advertisements (like your Sunday newspaper's circulars) and be taken directly to purchase that product. For the savvy Small Business owner to profit, this would be responsibly and effectively bringing this image recognition technology to a retail setting to enhance your customer's experience.

Picture a retail clothing store environment as a customer enters and is ready to try on a few articles of clothing. When they walk in the front door, a camera (perhaps the security camera already installed and activated) photographs the incoming client and the secure customer database recognizes her as a loyal customer. Within seconds, the store clerk on the floor gets a vibrating notification from the store's smartphone app letting him or her know to greet that loyal customer (by name) and to see if she needs any assistance. The app might search, theoretically, to see if the customer follows the store's Facebook page or any other social media profiles (and what she might have written in online reviews recently about the store or any related products). As well, it might profile several products on the floor that the customer would like and check whether it is in stock.

Now that the customer has selected a few items to purchase, she heads over to a few full-body length mirrors. But, they're not just mirrors! These are reflective displays where she can hold up the article of clothing in front of her and it captures the product, identifies her and then produces an image of her wearing the article(s) of clothing. (Refer to the end of Chapter 25 for the *Additional Reading* for the YouTube videos to see this kind of technology in action!) No changing room necessary! As she tries them on, she can change colors on-screen to see how she would look in pastel versus solid teal in this blouse, or chartreuse or olive in that particular dress. Her previous views are now thumbnail images on-screen also so she can do comparison-shopping.

Once she has selected the items she would like to purchase, she can use mobile payment technology (see Chapter 24's *Mobile Payments*) to checkout right there. She walks up to the checkout counter and they wrap up her items to go.

This sounds like science fiction in some ways, doesn't it?! On the contrary, though, it is most certainly science fact and soon to be reality in the coming years. As Small Business owners, you can adapt this image recognition technology in many different ways. If you are concerned about consumers relenting over privacy issues (even if it is completely lawful photography), you may use QR codes from Chapter 21 or NFC chips from Chapter 24 to recognize your clients initially instead of scanning them exactly. No matter the product or service, your business can likely use this tool to enhance your customer experience and improve your bottom line.

Additional Reading

• https://developer.vuforia.com/cloud-recognition-service [One development tool to research if you are interested in image recognition technology in your app.]

Chapter 23: Mobile Social Gamification

"You have to learn the rules of the game. And then you have to play better than anyone else."

~Albert Einstein

Gamification is a fairly new business marketing term, meaning to use the functions of games in controlling the behavior of consumers and employees. The history of games is a fascinating and much-understood part of human civilization's development. The ancient board games of Senet, Mancala, Go, and the like, give us a keyhole perspective that humans have always used play as a form of enjoyable, "deliberate practice" (the term pioneered by the research of the psychologist K. Anders Ericsson of Florida State University). It is this nature of using games to learn and hone skills from as far back as 3,000 BCE, that I tend to believe that humans developed play not just as social activities and leisurely pastimes but as a way to innovate, practice new evolutionary skills, and teach these to our progeny. So, when talk of gamification came to the tech community around 2010, I am of no surprise that modern business, with the tipping point reached of smartphone adoption in the world's wealthiest nations above 70%, that adding play to marketing was inevitable.

We all want our consumers to spend more time on our website, more time in our retail stores, and/or more time using our products or services. SoLoMo success is finding your customer where they are when they want or need your product or service using the most effective technology and marketing strategies. Gamification is encouraging, empowering and engraining in them the practice of doing it over and over again.

Of course, this could all be done in an analog

fashion with gold stars on leaderboards in shops and offices across America, but then it would be missing the digital technology component that is truly making this method gain momentum. I will explain this by talking about a passion of mine: language learning. I have always loved learning new languages. I happen to be quite good at picking up languages and I continue to this day being a "linguaphile" (lover of languages) so I always am looking at new resources to learn and refresh my language skills.

It was more than two years ago then that a friend moving cross-country who happens to be a neurolinguist mentioned to me this new Web app for language learning, DuoLingo [http://duolingo.com]. I did not give it much thought and reviewed the website and left it to the mental pile of "just another language learning website." Well, fast forward to today and I am addicted to DuoLingo! They built a mobile-social-gamified app for the Web, iOS and Android. So, I downloaded the app on my smartphone, signed up and logged on to the free service to learn my choice of Spanish, Italian, French, German, or Portuguese. I chose to brush up on my French. From there, I got introduced to my "coach" (a funky owl with fitness attire) who helped me set how much time I would spend learning my chosen language each day. In the app, there is a leaderboard, my lessons and exercises, and away I went!

A few times after I logged in, the app asked me if I wanted to play against my friends. I knew that my siblings were playing against each other in the DuoLingo app already, so I was not surprised. And a friend had requested to compete with me also, so I had requested to compete with a few fellow linguaphiles in the app. Well, the app has made learning language an interactive, reward-seeking and fun activity in my daily life!

I hope the pistons are firing in your creative minds as to how you could potentially use this technology to get your customers to get involved with your community, stay engaged in the discussion around your products, services or brand, and how you can get them to share it with their friends, family, colleagues and more.

Also, it is worth noting that advertising in smartphone apps that use mobile social gamification can also be really powerful. This advertising means that when unlock a "badge" or make the "next level" in the game concept of the app, it provides you with, let's say, a discount to your product or service. You partner with the app developer or the company behind the app, and pay them for you being one of the prizes.

Mobile social gamification is a rich and complicated toolkit for Small Business owners and it will take you some time to learn the in's and out's of how to accomplish this within your website, current digital marketing tools, mobile apps and more. But, if you decide to endeavor in these waters, it is an exciting and *tour de force* for the Small Business that gets it right. *Bon chance!* ("Good luck!" in French.)

Additional Reading

- http://appgamer.net

- http://slidetoplay.com

- http://theportablegamer.com

- http://touchgen.com

Chapter 24:
NFC...RFID...WTF?!

> "We're moving to this integration
> of biomedicine, information
> technology, wireless and mobile
> now - an era of digital medicine.
> Even my stethoscope is now digital.
> And of course, there's an app for
> that."
>
> ~Daniel Kraft

One of the most awe-inspiring aspects of the Digital Age is the promise of wireless connectivity. Everything we normally think about that was once connected by a cable, cord or adapter can now (or soon will) be communicating with each other via some kind of wireless technology. And while we have not quite (and maybe never will) completely be a wireless technology world, we will surely continue to improve and keep trying to reach that technological ideal. Naturally, there is an industry built around wireless technology, to which I would recommend *Wired* magazine consider re-branding itself as *Unwired*! However, my primary reason to discuss it here is to discuss its marketing opportunity for Small Business; **mobile payments** and **vicinity-based mobile engagement** are the promises of the future for our SoLoMo businesses.

Mobile Payments

You accept cash, checks, major credit cards, and perhaps even PayPal [http://paypay.com] or Stripe [http://stripe.com] for online invoices. We have all the ways to pay one another always at our fingertips, right? It turns out that's wrong. With the coming of the ubiquitous smartphone, manufacturers, financial institutions, merchant services, and enterprising startups alike all believe our phones should be our wallets! Even Google has dived into the mobile payments game. And for Small Business, that means you need to make sure you are preparing for the day when someone tries to purchase something from you and all they have in their possession is their phone. More importantly, you must prepare for the day when most people who come to your business desire to pay via their phone. Are credit cards and cash and checks going away? Oh, no! But like every new form payment we must embrace them in order to be and stay competitive in our industry. If this does not speak to you, I understand how foreign and misunderstood it can sound. But Small Business cried off pains and horror when credit and debit cards came onto the scene. Remarkably, we can thank them for much of our economic stimulus daily, weekly, monthly and annually today because customers buy with these cards more than any other method of payment. It's a great possibility we will look back on mobile payments the same way some day in the not-so-distant future.

So, what is a mobile payment technically, you ask? Well, the reigning technology has yet to be duked out. We have several opportunities and options on the market. The seeming victor is RFID (radio frequency identification) technology; these little chip readers are

embedded in your PoS (Point of Sale) register and reads from a special wireless chip in my smartphone when I acknowledge a purchase in process, usually with a 4- to 5-digit PIN (Personal Identification Number). In my opinion, with Android being the current ruler of smartphone activations globally, Google Wallet
[http://www.google.com/wallet/business/], Google's recent foray into mCommerce tools, is the best bet if your current merchant services does not have an RFID option. You will definitely want to check out the consumer functionality of Google Wallet also to see how it works for your customers so you can make the process on your side as smooth for both parties as possible.

There are new and burgeoning platforms jumping into the NFC (near-field communication) technology arena to compete with RFID, along with new apps that are trying to circumvent having to use additional wireless technology. Square, Intuit/GoPayment and PayPal have all launched credit card reader programs to accept payment via a small device attached to smartphones and tablets. While cool, I see these as intermediary to the real tide of mobile payment technology to remove the swipe and make the whole process "touchless." And so the Age of Touchless Payments will come. Will you be ready to eagerly accept your customers' money?

Vicinity-Based Mobile Engagement

The touchless payment model will foster another ingenious layer of information in which Small Business can swim, nurture and grow their customer base if you are willing enough to keep current with the technology. And yes, there is a possibility that Big Box stores and supermarkets may some day check your groceries out automatically, wirelessly, using RFID tags on all your products, and they will handle payment via your smartphone. But, by and large in the near long-term, we in smaller enterprises will not be shelling out the large cash investment in such mobile infrastructure. We can, though, take advantage of smaller, wireless readers that actively interact with and passively collect information from our customers (that they willfully give) while they are in or near our businesses. Want more Facebook likes,

Google+ follows, Twitter fans, or Pinterest followers? Ask everyone who comes into your store (and allows such requests) through their smartphone. Have a new special, deal, contest, promotion or coupon that you'd like to hand to every eligible person that walks in or near your office? You can do interactions like this with some available and coming technology. Now is the time to be developing your *think mobile first* strategy so that when the technology appears, you know exactly how you would utilize it.

Additional Reading

- The World's Most Targeted RFID Marketing Tool [http://goo.gl/2zpeQ]

Chapter 25: Augmented Reality

> "Social media companies must combine their mastery of the latest in real-time, location based or augmented reality technologies in the service of clear and consistent storytelling."
>
> ~Simon Mainwaring

This chapter is going to sound very futuristic, but I promise you that it will soon be a reality. Technology engineers are working on myriad ways to connect you to a computing device, in a manner that melds well with your biology. To explain, humans have limited means of collaborating (what we call input/output, or "I/O," in tech lingo) with a computer. For input, we can touch keys on a keyboard (i.e., physical keyboard or touchscreen display) with our fingers with pretty good dexterity, speak into a microphone with increasing software recognition accuracy, and we can gesture controls to command it from a device's built-in or attached camera. While for output, we can hear, see or feel (e.g., vibration) the computer's output from its speakers, display screen or body, respectively. For most competent technologists, they understand this is quite rudimentary biology with which they are dealing and design within these constraints. Further impediments to I/O are that as humans we say things we do not mean, use idiomatic phrases in our language, misinterpret data, and mishear frequently what was told to us (which is known as "selective hearing"). As I said about the Semantic Web in Chapter 22, computers creating data for us is one of the hopes of the future Web-connected experience, and can possibly overcome many of these conditions. One way for that to occur is through active or passive recording of life moments, whether speech-to-text, audio or video recordings. Not only have we seen the active recording of our lives come into reality over time with the invention of the Polaroid camera, then the video camcorder and now the ubiquitous cellphone. But, we are seeing more passive recording devices like the Muvi by veho, Siri (the personal virtual assistant built into Apple's iOS 5 and later), GoPro, Google Glass, and the many smartphone apps that track your location, activities and more just by setting it and leaving them running in the background. You can learn more about this passive tracking spurred by the "Quantified Self" movement; go ahead and Google it.

So, in line with this trend, I urge you to look through your Small Business lens to learn ways to take advantage of this technological future.

I will use one industry—real estate (e.g., design/build construction, home purchasing and rental markets)—to help you think about the implications in your business. If I were a real estate broker I would be building my website to include virtual tours of all my property listings (indoors and outdoors) and fill Google Maps with photos, video and whatever other rich information Google allows me to infuse the property with online. This way, once tools launch that allow you to build a virtual tour that your first client wearing Google Glass can take a live tour without you, you will already have all the available skills needed to streamline the process. First, I would get comfortable with recording my voice along with the virtual tours so that folks can connect with you as they view the property on their computer, tablet or phone. Second, I would test being on camera if I were comfortable talking about the property as though I were on a "green screen" like they have in video studios. Finally, pay attention to the entire real estate transaction process; who else needs to be involved and incorporated into the augmented reality experience of my client? I would start training my staff, real estate partners (home inspectors, settlement attorneys, loan officers and more) and myself on how to do these activities as part of my content strategy. More and more these are the presentation skills needed to take advantage of the augmented reality of the near future.

Again, I use real estate as an example, but you can relate this to the automotive, energy, manufacturing, agribusiness, retail and boutique shops, and almost all professional service-based industries.

Additional Reading

•   "A Day Made of Glass... Made possible by Corning. (2011)"
[https://www.youtube.com/watch?v=6Cf7IL_eZ38]

•   "A Day Made of Glass 2: Same Day. Expanded Corning Vision (2012)"
[https://www.youtube.com/watch?v=jZkHpNnXLB0]

Epilogue

"Action and reaction, ebb and flow, trial and error, change - this is the rhythm of living. Out of our over-confidence, fear; out of our fear, clearer vision, fresh hope. And out of hope, progress."

~Bruce Barton

You've made it! You have learned all that I can offer succinctly in this first edition about the New Way of marketing your Small Business on the Web—the *SoLoMo Success* way. When you began this journey with me, I am sure the idea of *SoLoMo* (Social Media, Local and Mobile) marketing was a strange-sounding and possibly overwhelming concept. Also, if you feel equally or more overwhelmed by all the possibilities available to you, I hope that the next few paragraphs will help allay some of those feelings. The Old Way of marketing for Small Business came out of a necessity to learn the practical methods to reach their target audiences. We grew up with these strategies used on us and we invested in similar ideas when we started our own businesses. I hope this book has helped open your eyes to the ever-changing landscape of Small Business marketing on the Web.

Remember that the New Way is an inclusive marketing approach of traditional marketing channels (from print, radio and TV advertising to word-of-mouth marketing) and new media channels that include your website, mobile website or apps, SMS, Web video and email marketing, and more. That is to say, do not forgo your successful, traditional marketing tactics until you have good financial evidence that it makes sense. All too often I see companies shift entire marketing budgets to new media approaches that are not yet fully developed, as an industry channel or within the business as a full-bodied marketing strategy. These are bound to fail and the business blames the platform or the technology or the staff or fill-in-the-blank. The blame shields the owner or management from the root of the problem; poor strategy was its Achilles' heel not the technology. Further, blame here is useless anyway. In any crisis (especially in business strategy which has its roots in military strategy), instead of crying over the car running out of gas, you start walking toward the nearest gas station before the sun starts to set.

It is when the sunset happens and you have worked a full day trying to implement some small piece of new technology in your business that frustration sets in. The possibilities that seemed endless also seem insurmountable in reality. Please take heed that in the world of Small Business less is more. If you feel the urge to try or do it all right now, please resist. I know much of what I talked about here is exciting and powerful technology and marketing strategy. I, myself, would like nothing more than to do everything I have discussed herein for my own businesses! But, I can't. And, likely, I never will. None are all practical for my businesses nor will my target audience (you reading this) would be interested in much of it anyway.

Honestly, start with one of these strategies in one of these chapters (starting with your local- and mobile-optimized website, most likely) and do that really well. If it is successful, you have the opportunity to continue on to the next leg of your strategy about six to nine months later. (Think about it. It took you about nine months to develop *in utero*, so should each new Web marketing strategy that you birth in your business.) Habits do not form overnight; they form from repeatedly doing the same, small activities every day. This piece of advice works for business marketing but translates for many areas of life generally: start at the beginning, bite off only a little more than you can chew at a time, and to quote the inimitable Winston Churchill, "Never, never, never give up."

And, while we are on the topic of perseverance, I hear quite often from business owners about their lack of interest in technology and therefore their lack of interest in keeping up with new technologies that I discussed in Part V. I know this is tempting but there are so many ways to help you stay abreast of new tools that will only make your business life better, that it hurts you more than it helps to ignore or disregard them.

Negative self-speak such as "I'm not good at technology" creeps out of business owners mouths when they learn who I am and what I do. I frequently bite my tongue not to respond with "So what?!" You learned to talk and walk, and you learned to brush your teeth and shower on a regular basis. Those two fundamental habits are the same as learning any new technology for your business' survival and ultimate success. I am sure most of us can agree that we do not like bookkeeping or paying taxes or working late when we could be spending time with our families. But, with the promise of a better life for ourselves and the ones we care about, we do it because it is vital to making our businesses survive and thrive. Take that energy you spend disliking technology, and commiserating with your colleagues over its difficulty, and use that energy to make an impact in your business (and therefore personal) life.

I will leave you on a positive note. I know each and every Small Business owner has a desire to make success happen in their company. You want to make money, sell your business, innovate in your profession or industry, and be proud of the work you do. You will need to target your audience through local search via your main website's content. Then, you will want to engage in a social way with your community. And, finally, you will want to interact with that same community wherever they are via their mobile devices and smartphones, while enhancing their customer experience with your brand, products or services. All the while, keep reminding yourself that you are talking to real people with real needs and wants. And, you are a person too, capable of making mistakes and doing great things without having to be perfect. Enjoy the foibles and mishaps as learning opportunities (as there will be) as well as the greater triumphs born out of your Web, mobile and digital marketing practices. Please let me know about them and I wish you the best in your SoLoMo Success and beyond!

Bibliography

21 Companies Using Gamification to Get Better Business Results. (n.d.). *Heyo Hub*. Retrieved May 2, 2013, from http://blog.heyo.com/21-companies-using-gamification-to-get-better-business-results/

Attention Span Statistics | Statistic Brain. (n.d.). Retrieved March 15, 2014, from http://www.statisticbrain.com/attention-span-statistics/

Baer, J. (n.d.). Should a Blog be Your Social Media Hub? *Should a Blog be Your Social Media Hub?* Retrieved from http://www.convinceandconvert.com/social-media-marketing/should-a-blog-be-your-social-media-hub/

Blog. (2013, April 21). In *Wikipedia, the free encyclopedia*. Retrieved from http://en.wikipedia.org/w/index.php?title=Blog&oldid=551465058

Cadwalladr, C. (2014, February 22). Are the robots about to rise? Google's new director of engineering thinks so…. *The Guardian*. Retrieved from http://www.theguardian.com/technology/2014/feb/22/robots-google-ray-kurzweil-terminator-singularity-artificial-intelligence

Cialdini, R. (n.d.). *Influence*.

Colvin, G. (2010). *Talent Is Overrated: What Really Separates World-Class Performers from Everybody Else*. Portfolio Trade.

Common Short Codes | Reach Your Audience with SMS Campaigns. (n.d.). Retrieved March 15, 2014, from http://www.usshortcodes.com/about-sms-short-codes/sms-marketing-examples.php

Covert, J., & Sattersten, T. (2011). *The 100 Best Business Books of All Time: What They Say, Why They Matter, and How They Can Help You* (Revised.). Portfolio Trade.

Coyle, D. (2009). *The Talent Code: Greatness Isn't Born. It's Grown. Here's How.* (1st ed.). Bantam.

Csikszentmihalyi, M. (1997). *Creativity: Flow and the Psychology of Discovery and Invention* (4 TRA.). Harper Perennial.

Csikszentmihalyi, M. (1998). *Finding Flow: The Psychology of Engagement with Everyday Life*. Basic Books.

Csikszentmihalyi, M. (2008). *Flow: The Psychology of Optimal Experience* (1ST ed.). Harper Perennial Modern Classics.

Ford, R., & Wiedemann, J. (Eds.). (2011). *Guidelines for Online Success: The Dos and Don'ts of the Internet from the best interactive agencies around the world.* Taschen.

Giles, D. (2003). *Media Psychology.* Routledge.

How to Create a Text Marketing Campaign | OPEN Forum. (n.d.). Retrieved September 28, 2013, from https://www.openforum.com/articles/how-to-create-a-text-marketing-campaign-1/?navlink=us-openf-brnd-related-content-2

Kerpen, D. (2011). *Likeable Social Media: How to Delight Your Customers, Create an Irresistible Brand, and Be Generally Amazing on Facebook* (1st ed.). McGraw-Hill.

Lemov, D., Woolway, E., & Yezzi, K. (2012). *Practice Perfect: 42 Rules for Getting Better at Getting Better* (1st ed.). Jossey-Bass.

Long Codes | Long Codes – one number for voice, text, pics, and video. (n.d.). Retrieved September 28, 2013, from http://www.longcodes.com/

Marketing mix. (2013, April 25). In *Wikipedia, the free encyclopedia.* Retrieved from
http://en.wikipedia.org/w/index.php?title=Marketing_mix&oldid=552084183

McKinsey 7S Framework - Wikipedia, the free encyclopedia. (n.d.). Retrieved from http://en.wikipedia.org/wiki/McKinsey_7S_Framework

Media naturalness theory. (2013, April 19). In *Wikipedia, the free encyclopedia.* Retrieved from
http://en.wikipedia.org/w/index.php?title=Media_naturalness_theory&oldid=526581142

Media psychology. (2013, April 19). In *Wikipedia, the free encyclopedia.* Retrieved from
http://en.wikipedia.org/w/index.php?title=Media_psychology&oldid=541279912

Mobile Gamification Done Right - Business Insider. (n.d.). Retrieved March 16, 2014, from http://www.businessinsider.com/mobile-gamification-done-right-2013-7

Mobile operating system. (2013, April 20). In *Wikipedia, the free encyclopedia.* Retrieved from
http://en.wikipedia.org/w/index.php?title=Mobile_operating_system&oldid=551350835

Pasqua, R., & Elkin, N. (n.d.). *Mobile Marketing: An Hour A Day.* Sybex.

Relation aller Fürnemmen und gedenckwürdigen Historien. (2013, April 19). In *Wikipedia, the free encyclopedia*. Retrieved from http://en.wikipedia.org/w/index.php?title=Relation_aller_F%C3%BCrnemmen_und_gedenckw%C3%BCrdigen_Historien&oldid=546814994

Schwartz, B. (2005). *The Paradox of Choice: Why More Is Less*. Harper Perennial.

Sociology. (2013, April 22). In *Wikipedia, the free encyclopedia*. Retrieved from http://en.wikipedia.org/w/index.php?title=Sociology&oldid=551546911

The ultimate mobile email statistics overview. (n.d.). Retrieved March 15, 2014, from http://www.emailmonday.com/mobile-email-usage-statistics

Tselentis, J. (2012). *The Graphic Designer's Electronic-Media Manual*. Rockport.

World Wide Web. (2013, May 4). In *Wikipedia, the free encyclopedia*. Retrieved from http://en.wikipedia.org/w/index.php?title=World_Wide_Web&oldid=553410556

About the Author

 Ray Sidney-Smith is a perennial Small Business Evangelist, working tirelessly to help small businesses launch, grow and succeed in the marketplace each and every day. He is the President of W3 Consulting, Inc., a consultancy providing small businesses, non-profit/community-based organizations, and small-to-solo law firms throughout the United States with practical approaches to business development using Web and digital technologies.

As a business and Web/digital technology strategist, Ray is often hired or invited by economic development authorities, chambers of commerce, small business development centers, and small business advocacy & support organizations to speak to SMB audiences, present technology workshop trainings, and conduct strategy sessions with small business owners on a myriad of management, Web and digital technology topics.

His work has focused over the past 16 years in the legal, small business start-up, and management fields. As a serial entrepreneur bootstrapping his own ventures, advising countless organizations and business owners, and sitting on the board of technology start-ups, he has developed a keen sense for what factors determine successful outcomes in business management and technology implementations. In addition to his consulting firm, Ray sits on the board of advisers for two technology start-up firms at any given time.

In his spare time, Ray organizes the two largest US-based personal productivity Meetup® groups (in Washington, DC and New York, NY) based on the books by David Allen, Getting Things Done and Making It All Work. Ray uses his education and passion for cognitive neuroscience, psychology, technology and personal productivity in working with professionals to learn the productivity methodology and supporting them at the different stages of their Getting Things Done (GTD) implementation. He produces weekly episodes for ProdPod, the podcast of productivity lessons in two minutes or less, hosts the weekly productivity Twitter chat, #ProdChat, and facilitates the popular Productivity Book Group.

You can connect with Ray all over the Social Web via http://flavors.me/rsidneysmith and on Google+ http://gplus.to/rsidneysmith.

www.ingramcontent.com/pod-product-compliance
Lightning Source LLC
Chambersburg PA
CBHW051759170526
45167CB00005B/1810